# Who Owns the Moon?

Other books by A. C. Grayling

ACADEMIC

*An Introduction to Philosophical Logic*
*The Refutation of Scepticism*
*Berkeley: The Central Arguments*
*Wittgenstein*
*Russell*
*Philosophy 1: A Guide through the Subject* (editor)
*Philosophy 2: Further through the Subject* (editor)
*The Continuum Encyclopaedia of British Philosophy* (editor)
*Truth, Meaning and Realism*
*Scepticism and the Possibility of Knowledge*
*The History of Philosophy*

GENERAL

*The Long March to the Fourth of June* (with Xu You Yu, as Li Xiao Jun)
*China: A Literary Companion* (with Susan Whitfield)
*The Future of Moral Values*
*The Quarrel of the Age: The Life and Times of William Hazlitt*
*Herrick: Lyrics of Love and Desire* (editor)
*What Is Good?*
*Descartes: The Life and Times of a Genius*
*Among the Dead Cities*
*Against All Gods*
*Towards the Light*
*The Choice of Hercules*
*Ideas that Matter*
*To Set Prometheus Free*
*Liberty in the Age of Terror*
*The Good Book*
*The God Argument*
*A Handbook of Humanism* (editor, with Andrew Copson)
*Friendship*
*The Age of Genius*
*War*
*Democracy and Its Crisis*
*The Good State*
*The Frontiers of Knowledge*
*For the Good of the World*
*Philosophy and Life*

ESSAY COLLECTIONS

*The Meaning of Things*
*The Reason of Things*
*The Mystery of Things*
*The Heart of Things*
*The Form of Things*
*Thinking of Answers*
*The Challenge of Things*

# Who Owns the Moon?

## In Defence of Humanity's Common Interests in Space

A. C. GRAYLING

ONEWORLD

A Oneworld Book

First published by Oneworld Publications in 2024


A CIP record for this title is available from the British Library

ISBN 978-0-86154-725-8 (hardback)
ISBN 978-0-86154-863-7 (trade paperback)
eISBN 978-086154-726-5



Typeset by Hewer Text UK Ltd, Edinburgh
Printed and bound in Australia by Griffin Press

Oneworld Publications
10 Bloomsbury Street
London WC1B 3SR
England

But this message was as nothing compared to their transformation of the moon. Hundreds of silver-suited workers with post-graduate degrees in astrophysics and low-gravity hydraulics drove their specially designed paint-spray vehicles between hundreds of kilometres of carefully placed markers, until below upon the earth could be seen the company name resplendent, fluorescent, and unmistakable.

[. . .]

But with the passage of time even the specially formulated paint could no longer stand the conditions of our satellite. Sprayed with lunar dust, battered by meteorites, expanded and contracted by extremes of temperature, the writing began to break up until it appeared that the face of the moon was smeared with blood. People would look up at the night sky, and shudder.

Louis de Bernières, *The Troublesome Offspring of Cardinal Guzman* (1992)

# CONTENTS

# ACKNOWLEDGEMENTS

My warm thanks go to Professor Daniela Portella Sampaio of Bielefeld University, Dr Kevin Hughes of the British Antarctic Survey (in his personal capacity), Professor Sheila Puffer of Northeastern University Boston, Professor Michelle Hanlon of the University of Mississippi School of Law, Bill Swainson, Sam Carter and Laura McFarlane.

I dedicate this book to the United Nations in admiration of its untiring efforts to promote peace and cooperation in a world too frequently reluctant to embrace either.

# PREFACE

Technological developments since the closing decades of the twentieth century have been so swift and far-reaching that they have already outstripped humanity's ability to think about how best to manage their impacts on people, societies, and the planet itself. Discussions are held and reports published by government departments, expert agencies, university research groups, and specialist non-governmental organisations, but there is insufficient general *public* awareness, and scarcely any public debate, about the ramifying effect of new technologies. Climate warming, and the ubiquitous application of AI in law, medicine, business, education, and the military sphere, have variously obtruded into public notice, though in the case of AI not yet with agreement about how its positive uses can be separated from its negative effects and how the latter can be managed. But gene editing, brain-chip interfacing, the harm to political systems and individual lives caused by abuses of social media – not least their platforming of deliberate and widespread misinformation – and the vulnerability of a digitally run world to hacking and manipulation, all appear to be out of control, with little public agreement about how they might be managed.

I discuss these matters in a recent book, *For the Good of the World* (Oneworld, 2022). In this present book I turn attention to a subject commanding even less public awareness: the reach into space by agencies, both public and private, planning to undertake commercial development of resources on the moon, on accessible asteroids in the local region of the solar system, and on Mars. At the same time, space is being rapidly militarised. The conjunction of potential for commercial rivalries and conflicts of armed national interests in space is a cause for grave unease; but it has scarcely impinged on public consciousness, or figured in public political debate.[1]

The prospect of commercial and military activity in space might seem a remote and even marginal matter, as remote in the future as it is in terms of distances; but it is precisely this assumption that leads us – 'us' the human community – to neglect making ourselves fully aware of the implications, and on that basis fully adequate preparations, for what is in fact much closer upon us than we suppose, and which on examination has its own menu of problematic aspects. Indeed the phrase 'much closer than we suppose' is already effectively out of date: in April 2023 the science journal *Nature* published an article with the headline 'Private Companies are Flocking to the Moon', reporting that 'a raft of commercial lunar missions are taking off in 2023', with the first of the new crop of landers – a Japanese craft deploying lunar rovers on behalf of the Japanese Aerospace Exploration Agency, together with others from the United Arab Emirates – scheduled to land on the moon that same month.[2] NASA now has a programme for commercial payload services, allowing companies in countries without their own national space programmes to send vehicles to the moon to explore and where possible to exploit resources. A Mexico-based scientist engaged in developing technology for these activities is quoted in *Nature* as saying, 'The future is there. You can consider the moon a new economy'.[3] A week later *The Economist* magazine asked, 'Which firm will win the new moon race? Three rival missions raise tricky questions about who owns lunar resources.'[4] The moon has arrived as a resource domain for Earth, and 'tricky questions' are multiplying.

On the face of it, commercial activity in space has welcome features; not only would it be better to mine minerals on the moon than on Earth for environmental reasons, but much will be learned from establishing settlements on the moon, and eventually Mars too, in scientific, technological, economic, and social ways – for they represent a new horizon for human experience, a new set of frontiers which will bring humanity the positives that exploration can offer. And in any case, commercial activity in space is already a long-established fact, given that much if not most of what falls under the description of telecommunications, television broadcasting, and remote sensing of various kinds, all operated by satellites orbiting in space, is commercial.

But second thoughts on the subject are less rosy. The expansion of human activity into space – beyond the relatively small-scale scientific work that has so far been done – might not be a problem in the way that colonialism and the relentless and unforgiving search for profit has so often been on Earth, given that the moon and Mars are uninhabited, without forms of life (so far as we know) that could be harmed by human occupation and industrial activity. But cynics would be justified in pointing out that the prospect of exporting humankind's less desirable habits into space, given its propensity for competition and conflict (arguing over who has exclusive access to this or that bit of the moon where resources are abundant or easily available, say), will all too probably cause problems back on Earth. We humans can be cooperative when it is in our interests to be, typically when the gaining of an advantage or the avoidance of a danger is at stake; we can be kind, altruistic, and self-sacrificing, especially on an individual level; but we are markedly otherwise, as history and common observation so abundantly show, when concerns of profit and self-interest – individual, corporate, or national – are at stake, showing how competitive, appetitive, jealous, and ambitious we can be, even (and too often) to the point of conflict and war. Are we likely to be any less competitive and ambitious when seeking commercial success in space, and along with it military dominance or at least influence?

There is, therefore, an important question to be asked: can we prevent space from becoming yet another but even larger arena of human conflict? What has so far been put in place, and what more should be put in place, to manage the already-developing activities in space in relation to their political, commercial, and military implications, to prevent humanity's less desirable proclivities from expressing themselves there, and causing major problems back on Earth as a result?

To answer this question we have to look at some highly relevant precedents. That is the aim of this book.

# INTRODUCTION

The region of space around planet Earth but above its atmosphere – the orbital zones – are crowded to the point of congestion by commercial, public service, and military satellites. Telecommunications, weather monitoring, GPS navigation, and broadcasting are by now commonplaces of the satellite realm, in 2022 estimated as worth US$350 billion, set to grow to over a trillion dollars in the course of the following two decades: 'we are now seeing the genuine commercialisation of outer space. Activities in outer space are no longer "out there" at all – they are very much here and now and play a major part in our everyday lives'.[1]

Inevitably, the military potential of space activity was understood early by states with the technical capacity to benefit from it. Space has already been designated a 'warfighting domain' by the US, China, and Russia; constellations of surveillance and communications satellites, essential not only to the command and control capacities of terrestrial military forces but to the monitoring of other nations' surveillance and communications satellites, have prompted counter-technologies; 'anti-satellite' (ASAT) weaponry, laser blinding of satellite sensors, electronic blocking of their signals, hacking of their control mechanisms to disrupt their flight paths – all this is now science fact, not science fiction.

In the twenty-first century humankind's activities are moving much further outwards into space, evolving from scientific to commercial activity in the inner region of the solar system closest to planet Earth, in particular on the moon, accessible asteroids, and Mars (not Venus which, although closer to Earth than Mars, has an extremely hostile atmosphere). By the end of the first quarter of the century plans for establishing bases on the moon were already advanced in those countries with the resources, technological and otherwise, for implementing them. It is more rather than less probable that human habitation of either or both the moon and Mars will have occurred by the century's end. Imagination can supply adjuncts to this thought, relating to industry, 'space tourism', and the multiplier effect on technology which would make the first tentative steps to human settlement of the moon and Mars a springboard for yet further human activity in the solar system – beyond, that is, the sending of small numbers of scientific probes, as has been the case since the first successful interplanetary probe – NASA's Mariner 2 – was launched in 1962. The possibility of accessible resources, even of life, on some of the moons of Jupiter and Saturn holds out just such a prospect.[2] The engineering challenges facing these more distant possibilities are considerable; but if the breathtakingly rapid and ever-accelerating rate of technological change in recent decades is a guide, there is scarcely any limit to what practically oriented imagination can suggest.

But imagination can also, all too readily, supply thoughts about the possibility of disagreement and competition, with the risk of the latter leading to conflict, among both private agencies and states active in space, disputing access to regions of the moon with promising mineral resources, say, or to areas of Mars most suitable for the establishment of bases or settlement. Indeed the precedents in human history make disagreement, competition, and – too soon – conflict sufficiently likely that before matters advance much further it is necessary to ask whether the nations of Earth can achieve genuinely sustainable agreement about how the reach into space is to be managed peacefully, without exporting to space a repetition of Earth's own quarrelsome history.

Another way of putting this point is to recall the concept of 'the tragedy of the commons'. This refers to the way individual actors (a person, a country) can harm what is supposed to be a shared resource by appropriating far more than a fair portion of it. Traditions of shared or 'common' ownership of resources, such as forests, agricultural land, and the water and fish extractable from rivers, abound in many places; prime examples are Germany and Switzerland for small-scale agriculture, Nepalese forests, Mexican irrigation systems, and Mongolian grasslands. In traditional English villages there is an area of land, indeed called a 'common', which all villagers have a right to use – the 'right of common' – for recreation, to graze livestock, to collect brushwood, to cut turf, and the like. If one of them overgrazes the land or takes all the brushwood or turf, it harms the interests of others, and inevitably the common itself. Similarly, both implicitly and explicitly there are assumptions about what humanity as a whole is entitled to regard as a common inheritance: implicitly, wildlife (such as animals on the African savannahs or in the forests of Borneo); explicitly, the open sea and Antarctica. Until recently the inaccessibility of the moon, asteroids, and Mars meant that no question was raised as to whether any person or country owns or has exclusive rights to all or part of any of them. Instead by default they have been regarded, if anyone thought of the matter, as the common possession of humanity as a whole – if indeed 'possession' is the right word; at very least it is accurate to say that humanity has a commonly held interest in them.

The emergence of nation states and their claims to absolute sovereignty within their own borders has given rise to serious dilemmas about the common interests of humankind. Despoliation of the Amazon rainforest is a threat to the whole planet because of its importance to the planet's climate; depletion of marine fish stocks, extinction of endangered species, and fallout from nuclear accidents or war are matters for which individual states are responsible but which affect many – in some cases everyone – in the world beyond national borders. Efforts to reach international agreements to protect what is of common value to all humanity have, alas, a highly doubtful history so far. This, therefore, is the worry affecting humanity's reach into space. Can the tragedy of the commons be averted in space? Can we prepare adequately for what will happen as the twenty-first century's technological and commercial race into space exports humanity's habits – so many of them bad – into it?

Undoubtedly it is better to conduct certain kinds of industrial activity, for example mining for minerals, on the moon or Mars than on planet Earth itself, as a way of defending Earth against further environmental damage. This is true. But if space-active states fall out with each other over access by themselves or their citizens to resources in space, and the disagreements escalate into conflict, the resulting harms will not be guaranteed to stay in space; a quarrel on the moon could easily result in fighting on Earth. Frank Herbert's famous novel *Dune* imagines conflicts in space over access to the valuable substance 'melange' – a life-prolonging and cognition-enhancing drug – which invokes with alarming accuracy the propensity of human beings to fall into fighting with each other over objects of desire.[3]

Some might say that these thoughts are overly pessimistic. Although almost unknown to the general public, efforts have been made since the 1960s – in response to the first manned space flight by the Soviet Union's Yuri Gagarin and what followed – to establish international agreements about space, the founding document being the United Nations' Outer Space Treaty (in practical terms a treaty agreed between the United States and the Soviet Union) that came into effect in 1967. But alas, the earthly precedents for these efforts' chances of success cause grave concern, for almost all international efforts to manage humankind's common interests provide examples of what has gone wrong, and what therefore can go wrong and almost certainly will go wrong in space, unless really secure arrangements are in place to avert it – binding treaties predicated on sustainable and fair agreements, well-policed with enforceable sanctions for breaches of them, would be among the most basic of such arrangements. One of many reasons to think so is that, more than almost any part of planet Earth itself, space is regarded as *terra nullius* – 'no man's land' – open to all and any. It is even more so than the shared domain of a Nepalese forest or the 'common' of an English village, a literal 'free for all'.

In the history of European expansion around the globe, planting a flag in a putatively unclaimed region and asserting a claim to it was deemed enough to 'own' it, for there was – in the view of the colonisers, and almost always wrongly – no one to gainsay. Is there no one to gainsay in the case of Mars and the moon? If local space, like the Antarctic and the world's wildlife each in its own way, is a common possession or at least a common interest of all humanity, cannot humanity gainsay?

This book is an examination of *directly relevant precedents* that give cause for concern about what might happen in space. These precedents are the Antarctic Treaty System, the Law of the Sea and associated principles relating to the seabed, and that particularly egregious example of European colonialism, the 'Scramble for Africa' in the late nineteenth century. Examination of these alongside an inspection of what is already in place in the way of international agreements about space will survey what is being done, and will illustrate what further needs to be done, in the way of thinking ahead and preparing. In *For the Good of the World* I discussed this problem in relation to climate change and technological developments which are outrunning our ability to manage any potentially negative consequences and the ethical challenges they pose. The focus of discussion there is the barriers to effective international agreement on these matters, none of which are manageable by individual states alone. The case of space is an even more dramatic example of this. As is always the case in relation to things human, one's inclination is to be pessimistic about the prospects, yet one must try to see what can be done, and to urge doing it. But first one must have a clear and informed idea of the problem.

This is not a book about the moon, asteroids, and Mars themselves, but about how exporting our too-common human bad behaviour to them might harm us back on Earth. At the time of writing these words, discussion about how to manage humankind's reach into space is confined to the small number of experts in the relevant fields of space activity. If there is not a much wider public debate about the matter, what happens in space will be decided by a few only (the governments of the space-active states, multinational corporations, mavericks like Elon Musk), and in their own interests – political and commercial interests, far from invariably the same as the interests of humanity and nature.

To inform discussion about how to manage humanity's commercial and military reach into space we have only one resource, namely, the experience of the past: the lessons it teaches and the warnings it contains. Since 1945, in particular, there have been repeated efforts to get international agreement on matters that only international action can effectively address – protecting the Antarctic, managing commercial exploitation of the oceans, combatting the effects of climate warming. All these efforts have been predicated on the bitter fact that without the restraint of such agreements the 'tragedy of the commons' will occur, which in turn will too likely generate conflict, even to the point of wars and the atrocities and suffering they bring. The history of scrambles for territory and resources involving past empires and more recent colonial adventures, replete with typical 'gold rush' phenomena of exploitation and rivalry, shows how necessary it is to discuss and agree on how to manage the next phase in the ever-outward and onward thrust of human ambition: the outer-space phase. This is why the need for a wider public debate is pressing, to ensure that what happens out there in the sky – with its rebounding effect on Earth – is not the result of a few heavily invested agencies doing what suits them alone.

This book invites that wider debate, and makes it impossible for our successors in our century and beyond to say, 'No one warned us; no one reminded us of what history shows could so easily go wrong when it is considerations of money and power that alone drive events'.

# 1

# 'GLOBAL COMMONS' AND THE INHERITANCE OF HUMANITY

The ambition to undertake mining operations on the moon was already advanced by the end of the first decade of the twenty-first century. Lunar probes had established that the moon contains many common minerals, including basalt, iron, quartz, and silicon, and the strong possibility that there are ores (minable deposits) of what geologists call 'incompatible lithophilic' elements: chlorine, lithium, beryllium, zirconium, uranium, thorium, and the rare earths.[1] Moreover, there are significant quantities of water ice at the moon's poles, the importance of which is that oxygen and hydrogen, the constituents of water ($H_2O$), can easily be separated to provide rocket propellant.[2] A number of private enterprises had already announced plans to market rocket fuel derived from this source, either in Low Earth Orbit or on the surface of the moon itself. One of these enterprises optimistically stated, twenty years before these words were written, that it hoped to do so 'within ten years'.[3] Although that is a goal yet to be reached, the barriers to doing so are practical only, relating to matters of finance and engineering, not to doubts about basic scientific feasibility.

Indeed the private companies involved – such as Shackleton Energy and Bigelow Aerospace[4] – were concerned more about questions of legality than engineering, asking such questions as 'would they own the resources they extract?' In 2014 Bigelow Aerospace asked the US Federal Aviation Administration's Office of Commercial Space Transportation to undertake a 'payload review' to advise on the matter.[5] (A payload review is an essential part of the authorisation process for any launch or re-entry of a space vehicle to examine whether it would 'jeopardize public health and safety, safety of property, US national security or foreign policy interests, or international obligations of the United States'.[6]) The question was important because investing in water and mineral extraction on the moon has to be guaranteed to provide a return if it is to take place. Yet as this shows, the focus was exclusively on practical and Earth-local legal considerations, not on any broader framework questions about the propriety of conducting commercial activities on the moon in the first place, or what would happen if conflicts of interest arose between different parties doing so.

The reason for the apparent neglect of broader framework questions is the assumption that the moon, Mars, and space generally (outside 'near space'[7]) is 'no man's land'. This assumption is explicit; in the relevant United Nations treaties and documents, space and celestial bodies are variously and collectively described as 'the heritage of mankind', 'the province of all mankind', and 'the common interest of mankind'.[8] These terms appear clear enough in meaning, particularly in light of the text of the Outer Space Treaty and its associated documents, which explicitly bar any public or private agency from claiming exclusive rights to any region of space, celestial body, or part of a celestial body. But in fact the vagueness of the expressions is deliberate, because they thereby avoid commitment to an interpretation in terms of the more precisely defined concepts of a 'global commons' and a 'global public good'. As we will see in Chapter 2 (in relation to the crucially significant Article IV of the Antarctic Treaty of 1961), deliberately non-committal phraseology is key to achieving agreement in cases where competing interests are in play, postponing the hard question of how to disambiguate or precisify them until – if or when – some crunch point is reached.

This strategy of deferring problems is, obviously, not ideal; crunch points have a habit of arriving. Is the temporary peace we achieve by palming off the problem to later generations as wise or as honourable as it might be? This becomes yet more obvious when we note that the Space Treaty of 1967, like the Antarctic Treaty of 1961 which provided a partial model for it, was signed in the circumstances of the Cold War, with the United States and the Soviet Union being chief drivers of it, since each was worried about the other putting weapons into space and using celestial bodies – as was their concern earlier in relation to the Antarctic – for nuclear testing. Discussion of space had been galvanised by the Soviet Union's success in achieving the first manned space flight (the Yuri Gagarin orbit of Earth in April 1961) and the race to put men on the moon, announced by US President John F. Kennedy in September 1962. Cold War considerations and the technology arms-race between the rival Cold War blocs were at the front of everyone's minds in discussions about space, not the commercial exploitation and human settlement of celestial bodies, both of which then seemed a far-off science-fiction dream. If anything shows how fast dreams can become realities in technology, the space story is the perfect example.

A necessary preliminary, therefore, is to examine the concepts of 'the province of all mankind', 'the heritage of mankind', 'the common interest of mankind', 'the global commons', and a 'global public good', to see what resources will be available for more precise thinking if or when a crunch point of competition and conflict is reached in space.

Of the two expressions 'the province of all mankind' and 'the common interest of mankind', the former is stronger and more definite, in implying that, to some degree, the idea of having a share in the domain in question – at least a right to access and even to make use of it, and to have a say about such access and use by others – is applicable. Indeed a right to access and make use of space and celestial bodies is explicitly mentioned in the Space Treaty and its associated documents.[9] By contrast, the idea of a 'common interest of mankind', which is as vague as it is general, carries no such implication. The survival of gorillas and elephants in the wild is a common interest of humankind, indeed a significant one which encourages campaigning and fund-raising on their behalf, but it carries no suggestion of an entitlement to (say) vote in the legislature of a state which is home to (say) a gorilla population in order to institute legal protections of gorilla habitats. Of course in an attenuated way this is not quite correct; a campaign in one's own country to persuade one's government to make representations in international bodies, such as the UN, to persuade and help a country with a wild gorilla population to protect that population, is a way of putting the 'common interest' into practical effect. But this is very different from being able to enter that country at will and to do things – erect a fence between agricultural areas and jungle, say – as of right, for gorilla habitats lie within the 'province' not of humanity but of individual states. If it were not a gorilla-occupied country but the moon at issue, then because the moon lies not just within humanity's 'common interest' but within humanity's 'province', all those who can fly there are expressly allowed by the Space Treaty and its associated documents to do what they like anywhere on it – apart from things military. The treaty requires only that any agency that does this must inform the UN and other interested parties that it is doing so.

The two phrases 'common interest' and 'humanity's province' in the UN Space Treaty and associated documents are far from the only relevant ones to consider. In other UN documents one finds reference to 'common heritage', for example in the United Nations Convention on the Law of the Sea (discussed in Chapter 3), while in theories of economics there occur the concepts of a 'global commons' and of 'global public goods', together with the technicalities of their definitions. All these notions are significant for understanding how the deliberately vague terminology of the UN treaties might come to be, or have to be, tightened when necessity arises. Moreover, this collection of ideas, and particularly their expression in UN treaties, introduces a very important novelty: the idea of *humankind* as a legal subject, that is, an entity in its own right ostensibly with rights, claims, and obligations.

The phrase 'the common heritage of mankind' occurs in the United Nations' 'Declaration of Principles Governing the Sea-Bed and the Ocean Floor' adopted by the General Assembly in 1970, picking up the phrase from discussion twelve years earlier in the first UN Conference on the Law of the Sea (1958), and repeated as Article 136 of the United Nations Convention on the Law of the Sea (UNCLOS, 1982).[10] Article 1 of the 1970 'Declaration of Principles' states that 'The seabed and ocean floor, and the subsoil thereof, beyond the limits of national jurisdiction (hereinafter referred to as the area) as well as the resources of the area, are the common heritage of mankind', and Article 2 states, 'The area shall not be subject to appropriation by any means by States or persons, natural or juridical, and no State shall claim or exercise sovereignty or sovereign rights over any part thereof.'[11]

This phraseology generates confusion, at first glance, for it appears to say that 'common heritage' amounts to 'common ownership' by excluding claims to any form of ownership of all or part of the seabed by any individual states or persons. Yet there is, on the face of it, a large difference between the idea of a 'common heritage of mankind' and common ownership of anything. The notion of what is in humanity's common ownership was already explicit in Roman law; the first section of Book II of the *Institutes* of Justinian, for a prime example, lists the air, rivers, sea, and seashore as being 'common to all by natural law'.[12] Before this the idea was no doubt generally implicit everywhere, in a not very populous world that was mainly wilderness and where appropriation to private or state ownership was infrequent. By contrast 'heritage', although denoting 'what is inherited', does not mean this in the literal sense of deriving actual ownership of something by (say) being bequeathed it – for a standard example, by being left it in one's parents' will. The latter is *an inheritance*; a *heritage* is more nebulously what people in the present regard as valuably continuing from the past, to be appreciated, enjoyed, or benefited from, and typically therefore as worth preserving. It is often associated with cultural artefacts and with areas of outstanding natural beauty or ecological importance, whether or not privately owned.

Accordingly, whereas the expressions 'common to all by natural law' and 'the province of all mankind' evidently mean the same in entailing 'being open to the use of all' – Justinian says 'anyone is at liberty' to fish in any river, tie up his boat at its banks, build a cottage on the seashore, and dry his nets there, because these places are 'the property of no man'[13] – they do not automatically refer to the same thing as 'the common heritage of mankind'. That is obvious in the case of cultural treasures and of natural domains which are especially valuable aesthetically or ecologically but which are privately owned. But it is not so obvious in the case of the open ocean and the seabed beyond national waters, because here the idea of there being a common heritage might expressly be that they are *not* available to anyone to use as he sees fit.

Note, however, that UNCLOS states, in modifying – perhaps going back on the implication of – the above-quoted articles from the 'Declaration of Principles Governing the Sea-Bed and the Ocean Floor' of 1970, 'the area of the seabed and ocean floor and the subsoil thereof, beyond the limits of national jurisdiction, as well as its resources, are the common heritage of mankind, the exploration and exploitation of which shall be carried out for the benefit of mankind as a whole, irrespective of the geographical location of States'.[14] The key phrase introduced into the Convention is 'exploitation' – principally meaning fishing, drilling, and mining – and 'heritage' has here been subtly transformed into a synonym of 'province'.

And now we note that although the UN's phrase 'the province of all mankind' and Justinian's phrase 'common to all by natural law' mean the same while 'common heritage of mankind' can at least sometimes imply the opposite regarding humankind's entitlement to what is thus described, all of them fall under the more general term 'the common interest of mankind'. Accordingly, the fact that something is a 'common interest of mankind' tells us nothing as to whether we have open season on it or whether it must be left undisturbed.

The UN documents are carefully phrased; the treaties are after all legal documents and when not maximally clear in their meaning they will be so for good reason – chiefly, for leaving open interpretations or determinations when evolving contexts shed then-relevant light on either. When the seabed Declaration speaks of 'heritage' and the Space Treaty speaks of 'province of mankind', what the former could be interpreted as sometimes forbidding or at least restricting, and what the latter is expressly licensing, are the same. The Declaration, having defined the 'area *and its resources*' of the seabed, sought to forbid both 'appropriation by any means' and claims of sovereignty over it, but not *exploitation* of resources found there. As Annex III of UNCLOS III shows, this quite different matter is to be managed, not forbidden. It is notable that in the public acclamation of the long-awaited 2023 High Seas Treaty aimed at protecting marine life (see Chapter 4; at time of writing this treaty is still to be ratified by the UN General Assembly), strong criticism was directed at the failure of the Declaration to achieve this. The Director of the High Seas Alliance (Rebecca Hubbard) said, 'Two-thirds of the ocean has just been exposed to the will and want of all . . . We have never been able to protect and manage marine life in the ocean beyond countries' jurisdictions'. In quoting her, the *Washington Post* added, 'International waters today are a Wild West of sorts, with little to no policing. Illegal fishing runs rampant and some seafood vessels even use slave labor'.[15] How inevitable is it that very similar words could apply to the moon and Mars in coming decades?

The Space Treaty says the same as the 1970 seabed Declaration only with respect to sovereignty over the moon or parts of it. The Space Treaty licenses commercial activity on the moon, whereas the 1970 seabed Declaration tried to discourage at least unbridled such activity; 'appropriation' applied to the seabed *and its resources* in the Declaration. But as we see, by the time the seabed Declaration had evolved into UNCLOS III of 1982, business and the economic interests of member states had achieved a remarkable evolution of intent, interpreting 'heritage of mankind' to mean the same as 'global commons' – in effect, the Wild West for which the High Seas Treaty of 2023 intends to be a partial Wyatt Earp. In all later treaties this elision of meanings is entrenched.

These considerations show that the concepts of the 'global commons' and a 'global public good' are therefore key.

Before turning to these two concepts, however, notice this: in the case of gorillas and elephants, the difference between what is 'humankind's heritage' and what is available to all humankind to exploit commercially is clear enough, but it is not secure enough, given that the profit motive has the power to override almost any barrier. In obscuring the boundary between, on the one hand, something that might legitimately be called 'humankind's heritage' in order to assert protection of it from humanity's customary profit-motivated depredations, and on the other hand a 'global commons' open to all to use commercially and otherwise, we lose a resource in the battle to protect some of the things we value from the relentless quest for money and power which, if it does not drive quite everything, nevertheless in the end determines everything.

And so to the concepts of the 'global commons' and of 'global public goods' themselves. The term *global commons* refers to any domain of natural assets that lies outside the ownership or control of any state or private agency, open to all to access and use. The standard list of global commons is: the high seas, the atmosphere, outer space, cyberspace (a more recent addition to the list), and Antarctica (somewhat controversially, but recognised as a global commons by international law). 'The high seas' includes the seabed; 'the atmosphere' includes airspace, in the sense of the region above Earth's surface where airplanes fly. Because of the fundamental importance of cyberspace to governments, business, communication, defence infrastructure, industry, transport, and so much more, security analysts regard it as an essential common resource. 'Cyberspace' is more than the internet; it is the complete environment of activity and exchange on the internet.

The resources of the global commons are defined by economists as 'non-rivalrous' and 'non-excludable' and therefore as both 'public goods' and, with the exception of outer space, 'common-pool resources'. As the quotation marks indicate, these are technical terms.

A good is *rivalrous* if its appropriation or consumption by one party reduces the availability of that good to other parties – for example, if someone catches lots of fish in a lake, there are obviously fewer fish left for others to catch. A non-rivalrous good is one whose consumption by one party does not reduce its availability to other parties; a good example is broadcast material – you do not reduce others' opportunity to listen to the radio by listening to the radio. An anti-rivalrous good is one whose consumption increases its availability to all – education might be (should be) an example.

An *excludable* good is one whose consumption is available only to those given access to it, typically by paying for it. A non-excludable good is one which is open to all either because it is too expensive to make it excludable, or impossible to do so – for example, the air. Generally speaking, excludable goods are privately owned, though publicly owned goods can be restricted to certain groups only, thus making them excludable. Rivalrous goods such as the fish in the sea are not privately owned until caught – exemplifying John Locke's idea of property as what results from 'mixing one's labour' with something, for example with some aspect of nature; this is an important point given its relevance to commercial activity in space – but overfishing reduces the availability of fish to others, thus exemplifying the 'tragedy of the commons'.[16]

A good that is non-rivalrous and non-excludable is a *public good*. Standard examples are what is provided by governments – defence, police and fire services, basic infrastructure – although private agencies can provide public goods too, for example information (through advertising) of the goods and services they offer. In none of these cases are the public goods free; what the government provides is paid for by taxation, and a private company's advertising budget is factored into the price of what it sells. In the case of government-provided public goods one might describe them as 'anti-excludable' because, to minimise the 'free-rider' problem of those who benefit from a public good but do not contribute their share to the cost of its provision, people have to be coerced to contribute – for a central example, by the government making it unlawful for anyone to fail to pay any due taxes.

A *global public good*, as the name itself states, is a non-rivalrous, non-excludable good available to everyone in the world, and it has the distinguishing feature of being free to everyone in the world, unlike most, if not all, more local public goods. A major example of a global public good is a healthy and sustainable global environment. Far more so than local public goods, however, global public goods have the unfortunate characteristic of being in short supply. They are undersupplied because there is too little in the way of incentive for their supply – people cannot be charged for accessing or using them; in most cases people feel only a small benefit from them individually; often the value of a global public good is only realised in the future, as with mitigations of climate warming. This is one of the chief reasons why governments focus more on providing local public goods – they can raise the funds for them through taxation, and they get domestic political benefit from supplying them – than in working together with other governments to create global public goods such as a sustainable global environment. However, the costs of failing to provide global public goods – the costs of allowing climate warming to increase, or failing to prevent or control global disease pandemics – can eventually prod a sluggish inclination into action. Even this provides no guarantees: as the history of international climate efforts shows, the action is often as sluggish as the inclination.

*Common-pool resources* are those which are both rivalrous (can be depleted, thus depriving some parties if other parties over-use them) and non-excludable (cannot be restricted only to some parties by pricing or other means, and are thus open to all). Examples are natural resources such as timber, fish, and coal, and man-made resources such as free bus services or (until 'congestion charging' was introduced) city streets. They are thus different from true public goods, which are both non-rivalrous and non-excludable. It is common-pool resources that most frequently experience the tragedy of the commons, for their non-excludability makes them attractive to exploiters, while their non-rivalrousness makes them vulnerable to over-exploitation.

From these definitions we see that as matters stand at time of writing, the UN Outer Space Treaty makes the moon a common-pool resource – the minerals and water ice on it are rivalrous but non-excludable goods. However, the moment these resources are extracted, they become excludable; they become the property of the agency that extracted them.

Immediately we can see two potential problems. First, the rivalrousness of moon resources makes a 'gold rush' phenomenon inevitable once the investment and engineering barriers have been surmounted. Second, both the Outer Space Treaty and the Law of the Sea contain the UN's admirable and always-iterated requirement that the use of global commons should be not merely sustainable but 'of benefit to all humankind', yet this requirement is at odds with the excludability arising at the moment extraction happens. In making the moon, asteroids, and Mars not global commons but common-pool resources, therefore, the Outer Space Treaty puts 'humanity's interest' in outer space under tension; for, as common-pool resources are the principal site of the tragedy of the commons, they are a common, frequent, and fertile source of conflict. One example is the repeated twentieth-century 'cod wars' involving Iceland, Britain, and Germany, whose fishing fleets operate in the North Atlantic; another is the tensions over access to and use of river waters in the Middle East and Central Asia (Turkey, Syria, and Iraq dispute their shared access to the Tigris and Euphrates; the Jordan River conflict involves Israel, Jordan, Lebanon, and Palestine; while the Aral Sea problem has embroiled all of Kazakhstan, Uzbekistan, Turkmenistan, Tajikistan, and Kyrgyzstan).[17]

If and when actual conflict occurs, the terms of the Outer Space Treaty and its associated documents will have to be revisited and their deliberately vague phraseology clarified. That clarification will involve more rigorous interpretations of the expressions 'common interest' and 'humanity's province' by reference to the ideas just canvassed. Doing this will require decisions about the nature and limits of permissible activity in outer space beyond the current ban on military uses. That is a matter of international politics; and matters of international politics are not well handled in a hurry, as knee-jerk reactions to situations that have already arisen. For this reason, revisiting the Outer Space Treaty well in advance of problems arising from its terminology is desirable. That means *now*.

If people think that the distances and engineering challenges involved in outer space are a reason for deferring consideration of these matters, they will be doing themselves no favours. The Outer Space Treaty, like the Antarctic Treaty, was itself a reaction to an existing situation, not something that was devised in a calm and unpressured environment of long-term rational planning. The situation was the sudden feasibility of access to space – Yuri Gagarin and the arms-race to reach the moon first, against a background of Cold War nuclear tensions – and the deliberate vagueness of terminology used, echoing the successful employment of vagueness in the Antarctic Treaty's celebrated Article IV a few years earlier (see Chapter 2), was a major help in making the treaty possible. But it is through a closer examination of two things, namely, how the Antarctic Treaty emerged, and how effective its subsequent application has been, that we see the stumbling blocks left by such vagueness. Add to this the similar problems of the Law of the Sea and the warning contained in the example of the nineteenth-century 'Scramble for Africa', and the case for revising the Outer Space Treaty sooner rather than later makes itself.

# 2

# PROTECTING THE ANTARCTIC

If a model is required of an enduring and successful international agreement, one need look no further than the Antarctic Treaty of 1961. The text of the treaty (Appendix 2) repays reading in full for a number of reasons, one of the chief of which is the emphatic commitment to preserving the Antarctic for peace and science. As an unspoiled region where there has never been war and where fraternal cooperation between nations engaged in scientific research offers a pattern for how the world's peoples should behave, it is a precious domain – and the scientific work done there has revealed how important Antarctica is for the planet's health. The treaty set a framework, which has been supplemented by further agreements relating to specific matters: the 1972 Convention for the Conservation of Antarctic Seals, the 1982 Convention on the Conservation of Antarctic Marine Living Resources, and the 1991 Protocol on Environmental Protection. Collectively the treaty and these supplementary instruments are known as the Antarctic Treaty System (ATS).

The treaty was drawn up and agreed by twelve nations at the prompting of the United States. It is not a United Nations treaty, though in the decades since the original signing a further thirty-four states have acceded to it. Of the total of forty-six signatory states, twenty-eight have 'consultative status' by virtue of their involvement in significant scientific research on the continent of Antarctica.

The enduring success of the ATS has prompted much discussion by theorists of international relations, whose interest in 'regimes' of agreements among nations is stimulated by the fact that the initial Antarctic Treaty emerged from a complicated situation in which seven states claimed sovereignty over tranches of the continent, and (with one exception) were reluctant to yield their claims, while at the same time no other states were prepared to accept those claims.[1] The seven claimants were (and *nota bene* are) Argentina, Australia, Chile, France, New Zealand, Norway, and the UK. Only New Zealand was, at one point, prepared to give up its claim because it then lacked the financial resources to maintain a research presence on the continent.

Recall that discussion of what to do about Antarctica occurred in the Cold War circumstances of the 1950s; it was the US and the Soviet Union (USSR) which were principally opposed to recognising territorial claims on the continent, while at the same time wishing to reserve the right to do so themselves at some future point. Accordingly the US proposed, and the USSR readily agreed, that a treaty excluding the Antarctic from military uses and nuclear weapons testing (though the US had earlier proposed it as a suitable place for this latter) should be sought. At the time none of the seven sovereignty claimants were in a position to resist the idea – France and the UK were recovering from the Second World War financially and were anyway in no position diplomatically, and certainly not militarily, to defend their claims against the Cold War principals. Moreover matters were complicated for the UK by the fact that although it *de facto* had an enormous territorial claim both in its own right and through New Zealand and Australia – the latter's footprint on the continent was largest of all, and the two countries were then still very close to the UK – its ownership of what it regarded as its own slice of the continent was disputed by both Argentina and Chile, which of course disputed possession with each other also.

Given that the ATS has been so stable to date despite the complicated circumstances from which it emerged, the interest of international relations theorists is understandable. Varieties of 'regime theory' – theories of the kinds of rules and processes by which international arrangements are created and maintained – are offered in explanation, their importance highlighted by the fact that the international domain is anarchic, and yet regimes manage to exist and facilitate relationships across the board from military détente to trade. At first blush it might seem that the chief reason for this is a relatively straightforward matter, namely, states' rational self-interest in observing the terms of agreements if doing so benefits them. Doubtless this is a major part of the picture, but regime theories show that the norms, rules, and procedures of a regime have an additional repertoire of elements, some explicit and some implicit, some formal and some informal, with a high contingency on context – such factors as prevailing conditions, historical factors, the expectations of the parties involved, levels of confidence and certainty, even the 'chemistry' of individual relationships between negotiators.[2]

One of the more persuasive theories discussed in connection with the ATS is Rational Choice Institutionalism, which suggests that agreements emerge from conditions of uncertainty when the parties see that compromising imposes less cost than maintaining their individually preferred outcomes.[3] Other theories, such as Punctuated Equilibrium Theory, premised on the idea that 'political attention is scarce and institutions are marred by friction, leading to policy agendas characterised by periods of stability, when there is little or no change, and periodic punctuations, marked by dramatic and rapid change', could be applied to the ATS as an example of a dramatic emergence of a regime out of Cold War conditions of instability or tension such as prevailed in the late 1950s; but it does not explain its continued smooth operation.[4] On the contrary, it gives cause for concern in implying that the stability of the regime to date is no guarantee of its continuing so – a puncture in the current equilibrium could, and on the theory probably will, occur when conditions for it are ripe.

This last point is especially pertinent given what was swept under the carpet by the famous Article IV of the Antarctic Treaty itself, the key article, along with Article XII, that made the treaty possible. Article IV states that the treaty does not involve a renunciation of any territorial claims on Antarctica by those among the contracting parties which have such claims (IV.1.a and b), does not prejudice the position of any contracting party 'as regards its recognition or non-recognition of any other State's right of claim or basis of claim' (IV.1.c), and that no discussion of the claims, and no new claims or enlargements of them, will take place while the treaty is in force (IV.2). The crucial feature that makes Article IV work is not actually in Article IV itself, but in Article XII, which provides that any change to the treaty can occur only by unanimous consent of the parties (XII.1.a), and that after thirty years from ratification (so, in 1991) a review of the treaty can be undertaken at the request of any of the contracting parties (XII.2.a). In the event, none of the contracting parties requested a review in 1991, and none has been requested to date: the efficacy of Article IV therefore – so far – continues.

Article IV is a quite undisguised, deliberate, and acknowledged fudge, and in its way a stroke of genius. By putting the sovereignty claims into storage it took the Antarctic out of the Cold War equation, while achieving the highly desirable aim of protecting the continent and making it open to all for scientific research. One key further benefit for both the US and the USSR is that it left open to them the possibility of each acquiring some portion of Antarctic territory for themselves in the future. Contrast this with the fraught situation in the Arctic, where the Cold War rivals were in close geographical proximity, making the region strategically significant in a way that the Antarctic was then not.

To describe the Antarctic Treaty solution as a by-product – a silver-lined one – of the Cold War is not to belittle the serious and well-intentioned aim of preserving the continent for peace and science; far from it. But a silver-lined by-product it was. The rival sovereignty claims might have had a different complexion without the realities of a tense international situation. That situation gave the US an additional motive for seeking an Antarctic Treaty: the seven sovereignty rivals were allies in the Western bloc, and the US did not want them falling out with each other. But in the celebratory tradition that has grown round the treaty it tends to be forgotten that this aspect of the US's aims was not wholly successful, because tensions between Chile and Argentina – and between Argentina and the UK over the Falkland Islands, sovereignty claims to which are related to Antarctica sovereignty issues – continued after the signing of the treaty, and at time of writing continue still.

To understand just what an achievement the treaty nevertheless represents, it is helpful to survey the evolution of the competing sovereignty claims that existed before treaty negotiations began. There were two principal initiating factors: the history of relations between Chile and Argentina, and the nineteenth-century global hegemony of Britain.

Chile and Argentina were born from the Spanish–American Wars of Independence, fought across the continent in the first decades of the nineteenth century. The prime mover of the independence endeavour, Simón Bolívar, attempted to keep the newly liberated Spanish-speaking areas of Colombia, Peru, Bolivia, Chile, and the River Plate provinces (later

Argentina) together as a single entity when Spain was defeated, but each region quickly asserted its own independence, triggering a series of conflicts over borders and territory, some of which remain unresolved.

For the Antarctic, of course, it is the border disagreement between Chile and Argentina that matters.[5] Determining where the border between them lies along its north and central extent was made simple by agreeing to place it along the summits of the Andes – the 'Snowy Cordilleras', constituting the east–west watershed in those regions of the continent. But in the south, in Patagonia, matters were not so simple, and even less so in connection with the islands in the stretch of sea between the southern tip of South America and the northern extent of the Antarctic Peninsula. Both countries took themselves to have inherited from Spain the ownership it had been granted, by the papal bull *Inter caetera* of 1493 and the Treaty of Tordesillas of 1494, of all new lands discovered in the Western world along a line 370 leagues (1,185 miles) west of the Azores and Cape Verde Islands (roughly 46°30' W of Greenwich), from the Arctic to the Antarctic. They regarded themselves as each entitled to claim whatever lay south by projection from the border between them. Fixing the border therefore mattered because it settled who owned the islands that lay beyond the continent's southern tip.

Argentina's determination to claim the islands and Antarctica was foreshadowed by its uncompromising treatment of the Mapuche natives of Patagonia in the 'Conquest of the Desert' campaign of the 1870s, designed not just to overcome Mapuche resistance to colonial expansion but to halt

Chilean expansion into the region. The Chileans were indeed attempting such expansion, having themselves defeated Mapuche 'Indians' in Araucania and assimilated their territory. As the Argentinian advance in the disputed region continued, Chile changed tactics and allied itself with the Mapuche, arming and supplying them, but in the event Argentina's campaign achieved its aim of bringing Patagonia under control and opening it to settlement. History has criticised the brutality of the 'Conquest' and some regard it as genocidal.[6] Given the stated aims of leaders of the military endeavour – 'to put down . . . this handful of savages' in order to secure the 'rich and fertile lands' of the region[7] – the charge of ethnic cleansing is hard to deny. It is not alone in being so in the history of both Americas, and so many places else.

Success in the 'Conquest' did not settle but exacerbated the border dispute with Chile. After the Border Treaty of 1881 establishing the Andes summits as the line, wrangling arose over its implication – as Chile saw it – that the key feature was that it designated the continental watershed as the border, and therefore that any rivers and lakes that drained westward lay in Chilean territory. Argentina replied that reference to the 'Snowy Cordilleras' did not imply the watershed, and that anyway some of the waters that drained westward actually originated in the Atlantic drainage basin but had been diverted towards the Pacific by glacial moraines. A resolution for Patagonia was effected by Britain in 1902, preventing what threatened to be an outbreak of war, by such expedients as drawing dividing lines down the middle of lakes claimed by both countries.

This did not end the dispute over the islands and Antarctica. An example is the Snipe Incident of 1958. Snipe is an uninhabited islet between Picton and Navarino islands in the Beagle Channel, the Argentinians taking the view that the Channel lies south of Navarino Island, placing Snipe in Argentinian waters. To cement its claim to Snipe, Chile decided to build a lighthouse on it, for the plausible reason that as the islet lies in the eastern mouth of the Beagle Channel it would be useful to shipping. The lighthouse was set up in January 1958. In April the Argentinian navy destroyed it and set up their own lighthouse. In May the Chilean navy dismantled the Argentinian lighthouse and replaced it with a new one of their own. On 9 June the Argentinian navy destroyed this new one by bombardment, and landed a platoon of Argentinian infantry to occupy the island.

War was avoided by a truce restoring the status quo ante: it was agreed that there would be no lighthouse and no military presence on the islet. This tenuous stand-off could only be temporary, so an international tribunal was set up at Britain's prompting to arbitrate more generally on the sovereignty of all islands in the disputed area. Both countries agreed to be bound by its findings. In 1972 the tribunal announced its decision, in favour of Chile. In 1978 Argentina rejected the decision and prepared a full-scale invasion of Chile under the speaking codename of 'Operation Soberanía' (Operation Sovereignty).[8] The aim had been to occupy the islands around Cape Horn and then proceed from there to invade the Chilean mainland at Punta Arenas and Puerto Natales, while simultaneously conducting an offensive through what is now known as the Cardenal Samore Pass in the Andes to capture Santiago, Valparaíso, and the region of Los Lagos. The Samore Pass acquired its name because it was Cardinal Samore whose intervention on behalf of Pope John Paul II stopped the invasion within hours of it starting, and brought the two countries to the negotiating table.

The long outcome of these negotiations was the 1984 Treaty of Peace and Friendship between the two countries, following a referendum in Argentina on a papal plan for resolving the question of sovereignty over the islands. In essence the resolution is that the islands belong to Chile but Argentina has freedom of passage among them. Two enabling factors for this outcome were Britain's defeat of Argentina in the Falklands War of 1982, and the election in 1983 of Raul Alfonsin as Argentina's president, the first democratically elected president since the overthrow of Isabel Perón in a coup by a military junta in 1976.

Argentinian sovereignty claims, however, do not fade away. After the Falklands War, which ended with the surrender of the Argentinian forces that had attempted to capture the islands, diplomatic relations between Britain and Argentina resumed in 1989, followed by a number of specific trilateral (that is, including the Falkland Islands devolved administration) agreements on such matters as fisheries, hydrocarbons, scheduled air services, shipping between the islands and Argentina, and environmental matters. But Argentina did not regard their defeat in the conflict as settling the sovereignty issue. In 2010 former Argentinian President Néstor Kirchner reaffirmed that the Falklands (for

Argentinians, Islas Malvinas) would one day belong to Argentina; in 2016 Argentina and Britain signed an agreement to park the sovereignty question indefinitely and to concentrate on further mutually advantageous arrangements. But on the sidelines of G7 meetings in both 2022 and 2023 the Argentinian claim to the Falklands was again raised, to be met by British insistence that the wish of the islanders to retain their UK affiliation was paramount. Argentina responded by withdrawing unilaterally from the 2016 pact.[9] At time of writing, therefore, this contentious question, which first arose in 1833 as Argentina was emerging as an independent country and extending its territories, remains unsettled. The British interest in the Falklands, South Georgia, and the South Sandwich Islands (and if one traces a finger up the mid-Atlantic northwards, the islands of Tristan da Cunha, St Helena, and Ascension) dates – at the earliest limit – to the 1690s, but became of increasing importance as British naval dominance required island possessions around the globe. Argentinian interest in the Falklands prompted Britain to declare them a Crown Colony in 1840 as a deterrent. The islands have never been Argentinian territory either *de facto* or *de jure*, but their proximity to the mainland and the richness of their marine resources have been powerful reasons for Argentina to want them.

British interest in islands because of its naval imperatives relates to the second of the factors mentioned above, namely, the nineteenth-century global hegemony of Britain. One of the features of this hegemony was that it licensed an assumption by the British that they had a stake, a say, a claim, anywhere in the world that was or could be of significance to their national interests – just as with the US after the Second World War and, at time of writing, is still so. In part as a result of the Chilean–Argentinian differences over sovereignty of the islands off Cape Horn, in 1908 the UK decided to clarify matters about its own claims in the neighbourhood by announcing, in the form of Letters Patent (a declaration, having legal force, by a head of state, in this case King Edward VII; in effect, a fiat), that in addition to the Falkland Islands it exercised sovereignty over South Georgia, the South Orkneys, the South Shetlands, the Sandwich Islands, and Graham's Land on the Antarctic Peninsula, an area lying below 50° south latitude and between 20° and 80° west longitude. In 1917 Britain further clarified its claim by stating that this sovereign area extended all the way to the South Pole. All these territories were designated Falkland Islands Dependencies and lay within the responsibility of the islands' governor. Already in 1841 Britain had claimed Victoria Land in eastern Antarctica abutting the Ross Sea; in 1923 it defined, by an Order in Council (another fiat), the area of the Ross Dependency itself, placing it under the authority of the Governor of New Zealand. In 1930 Enderby Land, a slice of the north-east of the continent extending to the Pole, was added to the claim. Victoria and Enderby Lands were transferred to Australia in 1933.

During the Second World War Britain mounted a secret operation, code-named Tabarin, establishing a base in its Antarctic territory, ostensibly to provide reconnaissance and weather data in the region, but with the added point of underpinning its sovereignty claim because of recent moves by Argentina and Chile to formalise their own claims to the same territory. Tabarin evolved into the Falkland Islands Dependencies Survey, now called the British Antarctic Survey.

One British politician in particular embodies the attitude realised in these claims: Leopold Amery, Colonial Secretary during much of the 1920s and all his political life a convinced imperialist. It was his view that 'the whole of the Antarctic should ultimately be included within the British Empire, and that, while the time has not yet arrived that a claim to all the continental territories should be put forward publicly, a definite and consistent policy should be followed of extending and asserting British control with the object of ultimately making it complete'.[10] Even if this ambition had been shared in full by Amery's colleagues, the realities were already against it, for in 1924 France established a claim in Adélie Land, a wedge extending inwards from the shore of the Southern Ocean to the Pole between two areas of Australian Antarctica, George V Land and Claire Land. Norway formalised its claim in 1939, naming it Queen Maud Land, followed by Argentina in 1940 and Chile in 1943. These claims were backed by appeals to history; the French naval officer Jules Dumont d'Urville had touched on Antarctica in the second voyage of his ship, the *Astrolabe,* in 1837, naming the Adélie penguin after his wife. Norway's Carl Larsen had discovered what came to be named the Larsen Ice Shelf in 1894 and established a whaling station on Britain's uninhabited island of South Georgia. And famously, Roald Amundsen beat Robert

Falcon Scott to the South Pole in 1911, reaching it on 14 December of that year.

Once the possibility of claiming the entire continent had gone, the UK decided that the best way to secure its claim was to persuade the US to plant its flag in Antarctica's so-far-unclaimed Pacific Ocean region. Despite the fact that it was a US navy officer, Lieutenant (later Admiral) Charles Wilkes, whose expedition of 1840 had established that Antarctica is a continent, the US showed little further interest until the 1920s, when it sent the first of several research expeditions, and in 1924 – the year that France laid claim to Adélie Land – stated that it favoured an 'open door' policy in which Antarctica belongs to no one but is accessible to all. The US's refusal to join their club disappointed the seven claimant states because, if the US had agreed, their claims would have been further secured thereby. The US's refusal increased uncertainty for them all.

The situation of uncertainty prompted E. W. ('Bill') Hunter Christie's book *The Antarctic Problem*, published in 1951. Hunter Christie was in a good position to see the difficulties at first hand. After Cambridge and war service, during which he was seriously wounded and invalided out in 1944, Hunter Christie joined the Foreign Office and served in it for several years before embarking on what became his main career as a barrister. While at the Foreign Office he was posted to the British Embassy in Buenos Aires where, to counter Argentinian claims to the Falkland Islands, he was tasked with researching the islands' history.[11] In the process he discovered just how uneasy matters had become in light of the Antarctica sovereignty claims made by Chile and Argentina during the war, while they thought Britain was distracted by fighting the Axis powers (their actions were the prompt for Britain's Operation Tabarin), together with Juan Perón's insistence that the Falklands be ceded to Argentina.[12] He was right; the two South American states' determination to prise British fingers off their neighbourhood and the Antarctic itself had its analogy in anti-colonial movements in India and almost everywhere else in the fading empire.

Although defending its title to its claims in the region below 50° south latitude was burdensome for Britain in its difficult post-war financial situation, a situation exacerbated by many continuing colonial obligations around the world, it was strongly resolved to do so, and therefore applied to the International Court of Justice in 1955 for recognition of its sovereignty claims in the region and for a declaration that the Chilean and Argentinian 'pretensions' were in breach of international law. Chile and Argentina adopted the strategy of refusing to accept the court's jurisdiction in the matter; in 1956, notifying that the matter had been withdrawn from its list of cases, the court stated that '*Des réponses reçues depuis lors de ces Gouvernements, il résulte qu'ils ne sont pas disposés à accepter la compétence de la Cour en la matière*' ('From the replies since received from these Governments, it appears that they are not prepared to accept the jurisdiction of the Court in the matter').[13] Had the two states been so 'disposed' they would have thereby agreed to be bound by the court's findings, and this – perhaps guessing the likely outcome – they would not do.

To make matters yet more fraught, post-war Soviet Union interest in the region unexpectedly increased. The US and UK had assumed that Moscow was focused on its vast Arctic territories, but its statement of interest, its refusal to accept the sovereignty claims of the 'polar G7', and its leaving open the possibility of making a claim of its own at a later date, were not only disturbing in themselves but increased the pressure on the US to restrain the claimant nations – its allies – from falling out with each other more seriously.

Into this tense mix came a timely rescue: a proposal for a year-long international geophysical project modelled on the International Polar Years of 1882–3 and 1932–3. The resulting International Geophysical Year (IGY) of 1957–8 was what made negotiations for an Antarctic Treaty possible. Those negotiations began in 1959, a year after the successful IGY ended.

It is worth noting in passing that the IGY was highly consequential in many ways. During it the full mapping of the mid-Atlantic ridges was achieved, significant in the following decade for the development of plate tectonic theory. Much was learned about cosmic radiation, gravity, geomagnetism, the physics of the ionosphere, and sunspot activity – the IGY occurred at the peak of the 1954–64 solar cycle – and more precise determinations were made of latitude and longitude. One of the year's principal legacies was the founding of the International Science Council's World Data System, a repository for quality scientific findings and a monitor of standards. Both the USSR and the US launched satellites during the year, the first two by the former, prompting the US to speed up its space projects by creating NASA.

Scientists from sixty-seven countries took part in the IGY. In Antarctica over half a dozen new research stations were set up, one of them by Japan. The success of the project, not least of the international collaboration which is one of science's chief civilising marks, created the conditions for an agreement to be reached on Antarctica, protecting it and ensuring its continued accessibility to scientists from all interested and technically competent countries.

The atmosphere of celebration that surrounds the treaty inherited much from the IGY's fraternal and collaborative spirit. But – reluctant as one is to introduce a sour note – behind the bright light of international agreement lurks the shadow of international discord, manifest even in the deliberate fudge of the treaty's Article IV. For as the discussion above shows, potential endures for the Antarctic to fall victim to the cycle of disagreements and conflicts that continue to bedevil relations below 50° south. (The Falkland Islands lie at 51.79° south; the Antarctic is defined as everything that lies below 60° south.)

Criticism of the ATS focuses on two principal points. The first is that it is insufficiently robust to protect the Antarctic from environmental damage. Preventing global warming is neither within the remit or the power of the ATS itself, of course, and nor can it do much about the seaborne and airborne pollutants that respectively fill the Southern Ocean with microplastics and the snow covering of Antarctica itself with persistent hazardous chemicals. But the fact that marine life is being depleted, with fish stocks in a perilous situation, that 170,000 tourists visit the continent every year not only bringing pollutants but interfering with scientific work, that dozens of private yachts penetrate 'sensitive' Antarctic waters, their occupants seen touching animals and flying drones over rookeries, are among the problems that the system is unable to address.[14]

This is because of the weakness of the ATS's governance arrangements. There was no central body to administer the system until 2004 when at last a permanent secretariat was established. But the secretariat serves the once-yearly Antarctic Treaty Consultative Meeting (ATCM) which has no powers in its own right, its members making recommendations to their own governments about any action required. Implementation of the ATS is accordingly reliant wholly on individual governments taking action, and the almost invariable tendency has been for them to restrict any actions they take to their own sphere of operation on the continent. Although the ATS mandates observation and inspection of all activity on the continent and in surrounding waters, it has no way of enforcing remedies for any breaches found. All that inspectors can do if they find breaches is to report them, leaving it to individual governments to take action if they choose to.

Of equal relevance for thinking about the moon and Mars is the second, related, focus of criticism. This is the ATS's vulnerability to geopolitical considerations. Antarctica is in danger from the persistent worldwide increase in commercial and resource pressures both on fish stocks and minerals crucial to advanced technology manufacture. The Antarctic Treaty forbids mining on the continent until 2048, but that prohibition holds only by the goodwill of the treaty parties, a goodwill which has been insufficient to prevent overfishing of Antarctic waters. Because the ATCM is a consultative and not a sovereign body – it is not 'the government of Antarctica' – it cannot assert and defend a claim to an exclusive zone for the seas and continental shelf beyond the continent's actual shoreline, as is the case everywhere else in the world (see Chapter 2). This means that the seas around Antarctica are defined as 'high seas' and therefore open to anyone to enjoy 'the freedom of the high seas' – hence the overfishing problem, and the danger of drilling and mining on the continental shelf.

In fact, the ATS is without control over anyone or any state not party to it. It does not prohibit any non-party agency from exploring the continent or exploiting its resources. Technically, all states are obliged under international law to support the Antarctic Treaty, but as resource pressures grow, and global warming creates more possibilities for accessing currently difficult or inaccessible resources, so the vulnerability of the ATS becomes more exposed. It has long been the case that parties to the treaty have pushed its boundaries – the 'non-military' strictures of the ATS are a practical dead-letter because GPS utilities at bases on the continent have dual civilian-military uses; for example China's BeiDou GPS, installed at its Great Wall, Zhongshan, and Dome A Kunlun bases on Antarctica, is designed 'to be able to monitor and support air and space weapons systems'.[15] But parties like

China (which became a member in 1983 and from 2014 onward has rapidly and significantly increased the pace of its involvement, developing and enlarging bases, building a permanent runway, increasing the number of Xue Long icebreaker ships, building satellite and telemetry installations, increasing its krill fishing activities, and in 2020 demanding recognition of its sovereignty over 20,000 square kilometres around the Kunlun base), have been vigorous in pushing against and – as this last point shows – beyond the limits that the ATS aspires to place on parties.

Indeed this last point – the sovereignty claim – is in direct opposition to Article IV and flags up what some commentators see as China's aggressive plan to become dominant in the Antarctic's future.[16] Both ATCM delegates and commentators note that China and Russia are reluctant to agree to initiatives that might hinder their future plans for activity in the Antarctic; in 2022 *Scientific American* reported that, for a sixth year in a row, 'China and Russia continue to block protections for Antarctica.'[17] This was in particular connection with the efforts by the Commission for the Conservation of Antarctic Marine Living Resources (CCAMLR) to extend protections over areas in the fragile Southern Ocean. Russia and China were the only two members of CCAMLR to refuse to support the initiative; all other parties were in favour. The report adds, 'The same two members have blocked similar proposals in other recent years.'

Those parties to the ATS who are less collegial in this way are evidently keeping their options open for the future, with an eye to the possibility of more resource extraction, and for making sovereignty claims allowing the development of the Antarctic commercially and industrially. The ATS exists to close down such possibilities; what we see here, therefore, is the old story repeating itself of individual parties curating their self-interest by manoeuvring to resist that aim.

One could add numerous other instances of difficulties that the much-celebrated Antarctic Treaty faces, but what has so far been said is more than sufficient to make the point that even the best of international efforts to agree on how to manage a 'common interest' (to put it no more strongly) of humankind is vulnerable to the all-too-common factors of commercial and national interests, constituting the expediency time-bombs that can wreck such agreements, and throughout history have so very often done so. The tensions that fizz just outside the margins of the Antarctic have not, so far, manifested in military confrontations on the Antarctic ice nor, so far, in outright and blatant violation of the terms of the ATS agreements on the continent itself, though in the decades either side of the signing of the treaty in 1961 the adjacent areas have indeed seen armed conflict – between Chile and Argentina among the islands off America's southern tip, and between Argentina and the UK in the Falkland Islands. The sovereignty questions at stake in these confrontations are not independent of those relating to the Antarctic continent itself, so the fact that these latter are merely in cold (to make a double pun on both geography and international relations) storage, and that other major parties have ambitions which increased practical accessibility of the Antarctic's resources will foster, shows that even this most celebrated of international arrangements provides no guarantee that the anarchy of self-interests which is the international order, and the resistless pressure of the pursuit of profit, will not overwhelm it.

The Southern Ocean is a fisheries resource, and is suffering the tragedy of the commons. Continental Antarctica has not yet become a field of commercial competition but, as the foregoing suggests, there is no guarantee that it will not become so in time, perhaps as soon as 2048 when the current mining moratorium ends. The Southern Ocean is an awful example of what happens when a common resource is open to commercial exploitation, and what might happen on the continent itself. It is therefore pertinent to consider the example of efforts to make the seas and oceans an arena of international agreement, given how relevant doing so is to thinking about what could happen in space. This is the subject of the next chapter.

# 3

# HIGH SEAS AND DEEP OCEANS

As an example of the problems that arise when a common resource becomes a field of commercial competition – then too soon and too often of heightened state competition, given that states are quick to assert and protect the rights of their merchants when the latter are threatened by rivals – one need only look at the sea.

Seventy per cent of the Earth's surface is covered by seas. They dwarf human beings and their activities, even their largest-scale activities. The vast expanse of the oceans, their depths – the phrase 'abyssal deep' to denote their profoundest parts chills the blood – the storms that rage across them, and the erosive power they exert in crashing against continents, make them seem invulnerable to human action. It is astonishing, therefore, to think that humankind has depleted the planet's fish populations, nearly driven whale species to extinction, polluted the seas with everything from microplastics to garbage and sewage, littered their floors with rusting hulks of shipwrecks and unexploded ordnance, made battlegrounds of them, altered their currents by warming the atmosphere, poisoned coral reefs, reduced marine diversity – in short, harmed the oceans in so many ways, all in the name of profit.

The treaty brokered by the UN in 2023 after ten years of haggling, unofficially (because at time of writing not yet ratified) known as the 'High Seas Treaty' – its formal title is 'Agreement under the United Nations Convention on the Law of the Sea on the conservation and sustainable use of marine biological diversity of areas beyond national jurisdiction' – seeks to bring about thirty per cent of the world's oceans under a regime of environmental safeguards. The aim is to create 'Marine Protected Areas', periodic meetings of parties to the treaty, and mechanisms for enforcing compliance with its provisions. It is an 'instrument' of the United Nations Convention on the Law of the Sea (UNCLOS) adopted in 1982, that is, a formal supplement to that Convention. The evolution of the 1982 Convention and the 2023 Agreement is an object lesson in the difficulty of getting international accord where economic and sovereignty pressures stand mightily in the way; both the Convention and the Agreement took many years to finalise.

The process of bringing human interaction with the seas under some form of law began long before UNCLOS – indeed, way back in ancient times. Some historians of law see the part of the sixth-century CE Code of Justinian known as the *Pandects* (a digest of laws and legal opinions previous to Justinian's reorganisation of the eastern Roman Empire's legal corpus) as preserving elements from the beginning of the first millennium BCE, because it contains references by the third-century CE Roman jurist Julius Paulus to the ancient *Lex Rhodia*, 'Rhodian Law' or 'Law of Rhodes', originating with the Phoenicians and governing shared liability in the case of losses at sea.[1] But it was much later, from the fifteenth century onwards, when Portuguese and Spanish mariners triggered a previously unparalleled degree of maritime activity in exploration and trade – the former in the interests of the latter, thereby initiating European globalisation, moving navigation from coastal waters onto and across the open seas – that made thinking about law in this domain necessary, because rivalry quickly made the seas an object of contention between maritime states.

The papal bull *Inter caetera* of 1493 that 'gave' Spain the world west of 46°30' latitude licensed the Spanish to regard the Pacific Ocean as their property, so they declared it a *mare clausum*, a closed sea, forbidding access to all others, even sending warships to patrol the Magellan Straits to prevent ships of other nations from rounding the Horn and entering it. This conflicted with an interpretation placed by Portugal on a pair of earlier papal bulls, dating from 1436 and 1455 and together known as *Romanus Pontifex*, which in the course of commending the Portuguese for fighting against Muslims and instructing them to subject any they captured to perpetual slavery, gave them the exclusive right to trade and fish along the coasts of any discovered land. Inevitably, exploration and trade along the west coast of Africa by both nations resulted in friction, and threatened worse because the Portuguese thought that the bulls gave them exclusive rights to the East Indies, while the Spanish regarded themselves as owning the Philippines (named for Philip II of Spain and 'discovered' by López de Villalobos in 1452).

By the early seventeenth century, with Dutch and English navigation well in the mixture, organised thought on the matter was overdue. The Dutch jurisprudent Hugo Grotius, 'the Father of International Law', published his *Mare Liberum* (The Freedom of the Seas) in 1609. The immediate prompt for the book was the Santa Catarina incident of 1603, in which a Spanish carrack of that name was seized by the Dutch off Singapore and its cargo sold for an immense sum. The Dutch claimed an exclusive right to the East Indies trade, having ousted the Portuguese and Spanish through a combination of diplomacy with local rulers and the size and organisation of their merchant marine. In rejecting the historic Portuguese and Spanish claims to monopoly in the region, Grotius, who was an advisor to the Dutch East India Company, argued that it followed from the 'self-evident and immutable first principle of the Law of Nations' that 'every nation is free to travel to every other nation, and to trade with it'. This entailed what he called 'a right of innocent passage' over sea as over land, though with even greater justification than in the case of land because the sea, like the air, is 'the common property of all'. The air is common property because 'First, it is not susceptible of occupation; and second its common use is destined for all men. For the same reasons the sea is common to all, because it is so limitless that it cannot become a possession of any one, and because it is adapted for the use of all, whether we consider it from the point of view of navigation or of fisheries'.[2]

This view was contested by the learned and controversial English lawyer and Parliamentarian John Selden, who responded to Grotius' views in his *Mare Clausum, The Right and Dominion of the Sea,* published in 1635 but written much earlier, in fact immediately after publication of Grotius' *Mare Liberum.* Selden's 'Epistle Dedicatory' to Charles I makes it clear that among the prompts for his book is the fact that there are, he says, 'foreign writers [i.e. Grotius] who rashly attribute Your Majesty's more Southern and Eastern Sea to their Princes', showing that the starting point is the question of sovereignty over territorial waters; but because the trespass on territorial waters follows from Grotius' claimed general principle of the freedom of the seas, Selden intends to refute the claim that 'all seas are common to the universality of Mankind'.[3] His argument was that there were no grounds for distinguishing between land and sea as regards claims to ownership or 'dominion', nor anything special about the nature of the sea itself that would justify such a distinction. For biblical support (though, interestingly, using phraseology specific to the Samaritan version of the Pentateuch) he quotes Deuteronomy 34:3, which describes Canaan as the land stretching from the Nile to the Euphrates '*unto the utmost sea,* or the *remotest,* which is the great or Western Sea'.

A compromise between the claim that the seas are free and the claim that a state with a shoreline has rights over adjacent waters was proposed by another Dutch jurisprudent, Cornelius van Bynkershoek, in his 1702 book *De Dominion*

*Maris* (On the Dominion of the Sea). This was the practical idea that a state could claim as much of the sea near its shores as a fired cannon ball can fly – a distance that came to be fixed as three nautical miles.[4] A combination of Grotius' view and the 'cannon shot rule' prevailed until the twentieth century's inexorable combination of population growth and technological advances rendered the compromise inadequate. The governments of some maritime countries, under commercial pressure, began to argue for greater controls in relation to fish and oil resources in their adjacent waters – the first offshore oil wells had been sunk in the 1890s. The League of Nations conference of 1930 (the Hague Codification Conference) specified the question of a legal regime for the sea as one of its topics, but no agreement was reached, the chief difficulty being how to define the nature and extents of 'territorial waters', 'high seas', and the 'adjacent contiguous zone' between them.[5] Despite the lack of definition, these concepts entered customary law and influenced the practice of maritime and flag states.

The need to clarify matters was made more urgent by the US decision in 1945 – quickly imitated by other maritime states – to claim jurisdiction over all natural resources on its continental shelf, which projected far beyond its territorial waters. In some cases the claims made by imitators were even bolder; the Pacific states of South America (Chile, Ecuador, and Peru) asserted exclusive rights to the fishing grounds of the Humboldt Current two hundred miles beyond their shores. President Harry S. Truman's 1945 'Proclamation 2667' (a 'Proclamation' being a US version of a British 'Order in Council' such as the latter used in claiming Antarctic territory – thus, a fiat) states, 'the United States regards the natural resources of the subsoil and sea bed of the continental shelf beneath the high seas but contiguous to the coasts of the United States as appertaining to the United States, subject to its jurisdiction and control'.[6] Prior to this the US had been insistent on the customary three nautical miles as the standard width of the waters – territorial waters – over which a state could claim 'jurisdiction and control'. But resource hunger – in particular, oil – is an exigent mind-changer, and as soon as the war with Japan was over (Japan formally surrendered on 2 September 1945, Proclamation 2667 is dated 28 September 1945) the US moved in this and other ways to assert its position in world affairs, with none to gainsay it: the victor's privilege.

The newly instituted United Nations saw it as imperative to formalise the new realities, and its International Law Commission set to work, starting in 1949, to draft articles as a basis for a treaty on the law of the sea. Negotiations among eighty-six attending states eventually began in Geneva in 1958 – the first United Nations Conference on the Law of the Sea (UNCLOS I) – and resulted in four conventions, respectively addressing 'the Territorial Sea and Contiguous Zone', 'the Continental Shelf', 'the High Seas', and 'Fishing and Conservation of the Living Resources of the High Seas'. There was an Optional Protocol on enforcement ('Compulsory Settlement of Disputes Arising out of the Law of the Sea Conventions'). But a significant weakness was the Conference's failure to agree on the breadth of 'territorial seas'. Accordingly the UN reconvened discussion of the matter in 1960 (UNCLOS II) and battle was joined between those states desiring a six-nautical-mile territorial sea and those desiring a twelve-nautical-mile territorial sea. Canada and the US jointly proposed a '6+6' compromise: a six-nautical-mile territorial sea plus a six-nautical-mile contiguous zone. The proposal failed by one vote.

Even as these discussions were in progress the world was moving rapidly on; decolonisation brought new actors into play, newly independent states with developing economies asserting their interests, requirements, and rights. Where UNCLOS I had eighty-six participant states, the continuing discussions of UNCLOS III that resulted in UNCLOS itself (the 'C' now standing for 'Convention' not 'Conference') saw 151 states at the closing session. A group of them, the 'Group of 77', proved influential in representing the perspective of the world's developing economies. In the years between 1960 and 1982 a babel of views emerged. Many of the parties were reluctant to accept the four UNCLOS I conventions, and meanwhile an assortment of local bilateral agreements had been reached over bordering maritime areas, a number of states laid claim to twelve-nautical-mile 'exclusive fishing zones' (EFZs), and some claimed rights over seas stretching offshore by as much as 400 nautical miles.

Another weakness of the UNCLOS I proposals emerged during the course of these debates; it had left the deep ocean floors out of account, because at the time there was no technology available to exploit its resources. But by the 1970s this was rapidly changing. Submarine pipelines and cables were being laid, and discoveries of polymetallic nodules (containing valuable minerals such as manganese, nickel, and cobalt) prompted interest in deep sea mining. In turn this raised questions about the seabed as a 'commons', because only those economies with sufficiently developed technologies could benefit from exploitation of these resources to the detriment of developing economies unable to share in an ocean floor 'gold rush'.

It was evident that the seas required an international regime of law that was fully comprehensive and systematic. The call was for a 'package deal', meaning one that had to be accepted as a whole or not at all, blocking attempts by individual states to enter reservations or to cherry-pick which parts to accept.[7] Negotiations at UNCLOS III, seeking 'a constitution for the oceans', began at the UN in 1973 and the resulting Convention was opened for signature in December 1982. It is a remarkably detailed and comprehensive document, enormously long: 320 articles each with its numerous sections and subsections, nine annexes, and two implementation agreements. It entered into force in November 1994 when the sixtieth UN member state ratified it (the state in question was Guyana).

Among those states that voted against adopting the Convention in 1982 were the US, Venezuela, Israel, and Turkey, all of whom at time of writing are still not signatories, in the US case because of Republican opposition in the Senate, where a two-thirds majority is required for ratification of treaties. This is despite support for it by the US armed forces and – recently – President Barack Obama and Secretary of State Hillary Clinton. President Reagan had at the outset voiced the standard Republican objection: that acceding to the treaty would diminish US 'sovereignty', describing UNCLOS as 'a dramatic step towards world government'. (That attitude explains Hillary Clinton's scoffing at Republican fears, in a Senate hearing on the Convention, that 'the UN's black helicopters are on their way' – an allusion to US conspiracy theories that the UN is secretly amassing an army to take over the US.)[8]

At time of writing the Convention has 168 signatories: 164 UN member states, the EU, Palestine as an Observer State, and the Cook Islands. Most of the non-signatories are landlocked countries with no access to the sea. Despite its non-ratification of the Convention, the US treats parts of it as having the status of customary international law, and in general abides by it. One of the strongest arguments in its favour is that it provides a resource for dealing with contentious matters such as China's controversial forward policy in the South China Sea, which involves militarising the Spratly Islands, rejecting claims by Vietnam and the Philippines about encroachment on their waters, and potentially interfering with 'innocent passage' of shipping.

A principal requirement for any sustainable international agreement on the seas, as UNCLOS I and II had shown, was clarification of what a state could claim as lying within its jurisdiction. UNCLOS defines four zones accordingly: 'territorial sea' up to twelve nautical miles from the 'baseline' coast (the baseline to be standardly taken as the low-water line marked on charts officially recognised by the state in question); a 'contiguous zone' up to an additional twelve nautical miles from the baseline; the 'Exclusive Economic Zone' (EEZ) up to 200 nautical miles from shore; and the continental shelf likewise up to 200 nautical miles (in certain cases up to 350 nautical miles). Beyond these latter limits lie the 'high seas', under no one's 'jurisdiction and control'.

A state's sovereignty over its territorial sea includes the airspace above it and the seabed and subsoil below it. A right of 'innocent passage' is allowed to vessels of all other states through these waters. The 'contiguous zone' provides a buffer for the state to protect the integrity of its territorial waters by giving it some rights of enforcement there. In the EEZ the state has sovereign rights for exploration, exploitation, conservation, and management of all resources, living and otherwise, both in the water column and in the underlying continental shelf. A further region of the continental shelf is available for resource exploitation subject to confirmation by a Commission established by the Convention for determining whether the state's rights extend to it. Beyond that is the high seas, and below the high seas is 'the Area', the seabed, a global commons administered by an International Seabed Authority in the interests of ensuring that a 'tragedy of the commons' does not occur as a result of technologically competent states exploiting the Area to the detriment of states not in a position to do so.

From the point of view of considering what might happen on the moon and Mars, it is necessary to look in a little more detail at certain key parts of UNCLOS, these being the Preamble, several articles of Part XI Section 2, and Annex III.

In Part XI Section 2 the articles of special interest are 136–7

'Common heritage of mankind', 140 'Benefit of mankind', and 141 'Exclusively for peaceful purposes'.[9]

Article 136 states that the seabed under the high seas ('the Area') is the 'common heritage' of mankind, and Article 137 defines what this means. The articles read as follows:

Article 136 *Common heritage of mankind*

The Area and its resources are the common heritage of mankind.

Article 137 *Legal status of the Area and its resources*

1. No State shall claim or exercise sovereignty or sovereign rights over any part of the Area or its resources, nor shall any State or natural or juridical person appropriate any part thereof. No such claim or exercise of sovereignty or sovereign rights nor such appropriation shall be recognized.

2. All rights in the resources of the Area are vested in mankind as a whole, on whose behalf the Authority shall act. These resources are not subject to alienation. The minerals recovered from the Area, however, may only be alienated in accordance with this Part and the rules, regulations and procedures of the Authority.

3. No State or natural or juridical person shall claim, acquire or exercise rights with respect to the minerals recovered from the Area except in accordance with this Part. Otherwise, no such claim, acquisition or exercise of such rights shall be recognized.

In the Introduction it was remarked that enterprises interested in extraction of the mineral and water-ice resources on the moon are more concerned about matters of ownership than engineering challenges. Points 2 and 3 just quoted show why. The paragraphs of Article 137 accept that what is a 'common heritage of mankind' is not always, and certainly not automatically, a 'global public good' to which anyone has unrestricted access for use or commercial exploitation. The point is reinforced by the words in UNCLOS's Preamble, stating that 'the area of the seabed and ocean floor and the subsoil thereof, beyond the limits of national jurisdiction, as well as its resources, are the common heritage of mankind, the exploration and exploitation of which shall be carried out for the benefit of mankind as a whole, irrespective of the geographical location of States', this time explicitly accounting for the interests of those states which are either not maritime states or are maritime states not in a position to compete for the treasures of the ocean floor.

Annex III sets out arrangements by which exploitation of the resources of the seabed are to be carried out 'for the benefit of mankind', in effect by taxation on the profits of commercial mining and drilling to provide the seabed Authority with revenue which, after covering its own operating costs, it can redistribute to parties unable to participate directly in harvesting the seabed's wealth. To understand the significance of this, and the controversy generated by the idea of 'an Authority' which not only controls who can do what in the Area but taxes their profits, it is helpful to see what is at stake.

From the point of view of commercial prospects in the Area, it is the deep seabed, below 200 metres depth, covering nearly two-thirds of the total, that is of special interest. This is because reserves of copper, aluminium, nickel, zinc, manganese, cobalt, and lithium available on land are diminishing, so deep sea mining has become financially attractive – for even as land sources of these metals decrease, demand for them in the technologies of smartphones, solar panels, wind turbines, laser crystals, and batteries is increasing. These technologies are of more recent date than the first recognition of potential resources under the waves; the geologist John L. Mero's 1965 book *The Mineral Resources of the Sea* sounded the alert, and was the prompt for UN endeavours to claim the ocean's wealth for all humanity.[10] A significant, and appropriate, factor was the political climate of the 1960s: on the one hand there was decolonisation, the emergence of new states and nations far behind in economic development terms than the handful of leading economies, and sensitivity to the rights of peoples and of minorities, and on the other hand there was the tense Cold War stand-off that brought urgency to removing as many potentials for conflict as possible and sequestering them in a neutral shared worldwide domain – the Antarctic, space, and the high seas and their seabed being prime examples.

Malta's ambassador to the UN at the time Mero's book was published was Arvid Pardo, who was prompted by it to urge the UN to lay claim to the seabed as a possession of all humanity. It was this that prompted adoption in 1970 of UN Resolution 2749, the 'Declaration of Principles Governing the Sea-Bed and the Ocean Floor' already mentioned. Perhaps fortunately for the proceedings that led to UNCLOS, the following decade saw a collapse in worldwide metal prices, making seabed mining uneconomic, and the new technologies with their hunger for lithium and other necessary metals were still only ramping up when the Seabed Authority came into existence in 1994, the date of ratification of UNCLOS thus bringing it into effect. For those concerned about the seas and seabed, this was a moment of celebration. Three decades later the International Seabed Authority could claim success:

> This legal mechanism was established to prevent a scramble for the resources of the seabed by the technologically advanced countries and to ensure that activities carried out in that space (marine scientific research, exploration, exploitation) would benefit humankind as a whole through the equitable sharing of financial and economic benefits with the international community, in particular. In the alternative, access to those mineral resources would have been on a first-come, first-served basis without international management.[11]

Although this breathing space allowed the Convention and Authority to be born, both were (and are) far from uncontroversial. The most significant reason for this is UNCLOS making it a legal obligation that seabed exploration and exploitation only be undertaken with permission from the International Seabed Authority, and that when commercial exploitation of the seabed occurs, royalties must be paid to it.

The chief objector to these arrangements is the US. Its main claim is that even if it chose to observe, without acceding to, the UNCLOS principles, the only restriction on it would be to not claim sovereignty over any part of the high seas or their seabed, and to conduct activities there with due regard to the rights of others involved in exploration or exploitation. The US's own 'Deep Seabed Hard Mineral Resource Act' (1980 – note the date; it was designed to pre-empt UNCLOS) is the only authority its own commercial operators recognise.

In justification, defenders of the US's position point out that there is little risk of conflicts between entities of different nations engaged in deep sea mining, given the vast extent of the oceans and the localised nature of mining, so no international authority is needed to control mining activities. There is also the fact that companies like Lockheed Martin had obtained their licences for deep seabed mining before UNCLOS and therefore had 'legacy claims' predating the Law of the Sea. And there were bilateral agreements in force with other states covering extraction operations before UNCLOS too. Accordingly, so the argument concludes, there is no good reason for there to be a UNCLOS and its International Seabed Authority, and certainly no good reason for the US to recognise either.[12]

On the other side of the argument it is pointed out that the enormous expense of seabed mining puts investment by US firms in question, for fear of legal disputes being brought by other states invoking UNCLOS provisions. One of the advocates for the US joining UNCLOS, J. N. Moore, said in his submission to the Senate Foreign Relations Committee,

'Paradoxically, "protecting" our deep seabed industry has sometimes been a mantra for non-adherence to the Convention. Yet because of uncertainties resulting from US non-adherence these sites have been virtually abandoned and most of our nascent deep seabed mining industry has disappeared. Moreover, it is clear that without US adherence to the Convention our industry has absolutely no chance of being revived.'[13] The last claim might be questioned on the grounds that drilling and mining on the continental shelf and within the US's EEZ are not vulnerable to UNCLOS-invoking challenges, so although a *deep* seabed mining industry in 'the Area' might be subject to inhibitions for this reason – and therefore to loss of opportunity in developing relevant technologies and accessing valuable resources – the industry is not completely hollowed out by non-accession. Still, some of the most valued potential resources are found only on the deep seabed, and if Moore is right, the US's non-accession indeed constitutes a barrier.

As of November 2021 the International Seabed Authority had signed thirty-one contracts with twenty-one different state parties, eleven of them states with developing economies. These are small numbers, and are a reflection of the slow progress so far made in the relevant technologies and the tentative degree of financial commitment to the deep sea mining sector. As with outer space, one can expect a tipping-point to be reached at which a conjunction of technological feasibility, need, and the availability of finance precipitate a rush. With UNCLOS and the International Seabed Authority there is a significant degree of preparation in the way of framework and mechanisms in place; but with major possible players refusing to recognise them, the risk of breakdown of the arrangements is real – not least because of the perennial problem of *enforcement*. The fact that UNCLOS sees the seabed as an arena for commercial exploitation, and that its control over what happens there is dependent on the willingness of signatory parties to accept the authority of the International Seabed Authority, identifies the crucial point of weakness, most especially because those who refuse to subscribe to UNCLOS see the Authority's ambitions as an unwarranted intervention in what is or should be a genuine global common.

This latter is the US's position. To them what is as a red rag to a bull is Annex III of UNCLOS.

Annex III sets out the process required for any state or private enterprise to get the International Seabed Authority's approval to carry out prospecting in the Area. For exploiting resources in the Area, the International Seabed Authority requires detailed plans of work including methods and equipment, assurances about compliance with UNCLOS regulations, and assessment of impacts on the marine environment. An applicant entity has to be suitably qualified, and must be sponsored by a state party to UNCLOS and subject to its laws. The application fees and subsequent annual fixed fee are significant, in the currently available version of Annex III stated to be $500,000 for an application and £1,000,000 per annum respectively. If the extractor's earnings yield a 'production charge' greater than the fixed fee, then the higher of the two sums has to be paid, the royalty exacted by the

International Seabed Authority consisting in various percentages (from five to seventy per cent) of net proceeds.[14] The International Seabed Authority's control of all aspects of what happens in exploration and exploitation in the Area is extensive and comprehensive; Article 17 of the Annex gives a long list of them.

Critics of UNCLOS see this as an expensive bureaucracy trespassing on and interfering in a global common. Defenders point to the endeavour to make a global common genuinely of benefit to all and not just to those who happen to be best placed to – perhaps – wreak a tragedy of the commons upon it.

And they would also point to the mention, though it is a passing one, to the International Seabed Authority requiring information about impacts of exploration and exploitation on the marine environment. A major concern for environmentalists is the damage that mining will cause to ocean ecosystems. Different metal deposits are found at different depths, so nowhere in the ocean is safe. Cobalt crusts are found on seamounts, accessible at 1,000 metres depth; polymetallic sulphides ('sea floor massive sulphides') are found on mid-ocean ridges at 2,000 metres depth; ferromanganese crusts and polymetallic nodules lie on the abyssal plains at 5,000 metres depth. Drilling will at least disturb, and at worst destroy, the areas themselves, generate plumes of waste and sediment in the water column compromising respiration and feeding of marine creatures, cause noise that will stress and disorientate them, and damage the ecological balance of the living organisms within the radius of the exploited region.[15]

These concerns will almost certainly not apply to the moon and Mars, but if life is found on some of the moons of Saturn and Jupiter (Saturn's Titan and Enceladus are candidates of interest, as are Jupiter's Galilean moons), which is now thought possible, then – given that activity on the moon and Mars will further enable access to other regions of the solar system – thought will need to be given to protecting it in ways far more effective than now exists for Earth's oceans.

A final point of interest in UNCLOS is the International Tribunal for the Law of the Sea whose constitution and functions are set out in Annex VI. For anyone interested in whether UNCLOS has teeth, Article 39 is key; it states that decisions relating to the seabed 'shall be enforceable in the territories of the States Parties in the same manner as judgments or orders of the highest court of the State Party in whose territory the enforcement is sought.'[16] Critics take the view that this is a trespass on national sovereignty, of a piece with the entire tendency of UNCLOS to be so. The resource available to defenders is that if state parties to UNCLOS are serious about their commitment, it would be in their interests to see the decisions of the tribunal enforced, and accordingly to act in ways that would make enforcement happen.

Along with the Antarctic, though in a more complicated way, the oceans are the closest analogue to outer space that we have as a source for comparisons. Efforts to bring the oceans under international agreement are arguably an even closer analogue to what is needful in regard to space. For whereas the Antarctic Treaty is not a UN instrument, but an agreement between a group of nations at that time either of leading significance in the world or of geographical accident, UNCLOS is a major international effort to provide a thoroughly worked-out framework for the world's most shared common domain. In comparison to UNCLOS's extent, breadth, and depth, the current UN Outer Space Treaty and its associated instruments look positively meagre. That is a function of the nascent condition of exploration – and certainly of exploitation – of the moon, asteroids, and Mars at time of writing. But given the tipping-point consideration about technology, investment, and need coming together in circumstances of depleting resources, a tipping-point as imminent in the outer space case as with the seabed, the question is: is it not time to consider a version of the Outer Space Treaty far closer to UNCLOS? For if a tipping-point is reached and a scramble for the moon begins, a *post facto* effort to manage it in the interests of avoiding conflict will be much harder, a fact that consideration of gold-rush-type scrambles such as the Scramble for Africa – the subject of the next chapter – all too well illustrate.[17]

# 4

# THE SCRAMBLE FOR AFRICA

There are many examples – too many – of 'scrambles' for profit and advantage in the history of globalisation. In India and the East Indies, in Central and South America, in the gold rushes of North America and Australia, in the forced appropriation of land and control in all those places, and in European imposition of trade bases and extraterritoriality conditions on a reluctant nineteenth-century China, lies the proof that the opening of new frontiers always carries at least the potential, if not indeed the inevitability, of conflict. The new frontier of space differs from these examples in the crucial respect that there are no populations of sentient beings on the moon and Mars – so far as we know – whose interests would be harmed by exploitation of natural resources found there, and especially by competitive such exploitation. But in the history of globalisation, conflict did not occur only between the globalisers and the people they imposed upon, but among globalisers themselves, competing in the scramble to be first or to get most. This is the lesson of history that applies directly to the coming expansion of human activity in space.

One might choose from a number of examples of scrambles to hear the warning note they sound. Think of what happened when gold was discovered in the Pikes Peak area of the Rocky Mountains in Colorado in 1858. Seven years earlier the US government had signed a treaty at Fort Laramie with the Cheyenne, Arapaho, and five other 'Indian nations' recognising their right to the lands between the North Platte River and the Arkansas River, an enormous tract of territory covering parts of what are now the states of Wyoming, Nebraska, Kansas, and Colorado itself. With the rush of prospectors and settlers into the region came demands for the government to revise the Fort Laramie treaty with a view to limiting the extent of Native American land. The result was that eleven-twelfths of the lands recognised at Fort Laramie were taken from the Native Americans, prompting a violent reaction. Warrior bands of Cheyenne 'Dog Soldiers' attacked settlers, and indiscriminate reprisals against the tribes, including those who were peaceful, reached their apogee in incidents like the brutal massacre of Native Americans, mainly women and children, at Sand Creek in 1864.[1] Nor, in the prevailing 'Wild West' conditions, were the arriving folk themselves a peaceful population; jostling for advantage in the 'public common' – the *terra nullius* as they viewed it – of the new lands saw inevitable conflicts arise.[2]

Allowing for the difference between the Colorado and moon cases, the lesson of the example is that hunger for gold – for profit – trumps concern for just about anything else, including human life. If gold or its contemporary equivalents in rare metals or other much-desired resources are found on the moon – remember *Dune*'s example of 'melange' – a high-tech version both of a gold rush and of potential for conflict would all too likely ensue. What has already been found on the moon is enough to whet commercial appetite.

The most flagrant example of private and state-sponsored scrambles is without question the 'Scramble for Africa' in the last decades of the nineteenth century. The examples mentioned at the beginning of this chapter pale in comparison to the appropriation, in less than three decades, of most of an entire continent, ten million square miles of territory treated as if it were empty land, with 110 million inhabitants treated as if they were not there in any political, and scarcely in any moral, sense.

At the time that the famous Africa explorer David Livingstone died in 1873, at Chipundu in what is now Zambia, Africa was still in European eyes 'the Dark Continent', its interior 'unknown' except to a handful of explorers, who were alone conscious of the fact that Africa was well enough known to the tens of millions of people who lived there, in complex societies with long histories.[3] But the native inhabitants of Africa were, in the view of most people outside the continent, a kind of nonentity, 'natives' living in primitive conditions, later regarded – when the Scramble began in earnest – as merely instrumental (though occasionally a hindrance) to European objectives.

Wholly different from the oblivious kind of non-African incomer, Livingstone liked and was liked by the people he met in his long journeys through the southern and south-central regions of the continent, his most famous journey starting (to use contemporary names) on the eastern seaboard of Mozambique and taking him up the Zambezi River, across to Angola and back, through Zambia and Malawi, up beyond the Bangweulu swamps and Lake Mweru to the Lualaba River and across to Lake Tanganyika; an immense terrain, varied in its peoples, its tropical diseases devastating to Europeans, and at the time plagued by the slave trade serving the Arab and Ottoman parts of the world.

Livingstone was a medical doctor and a missionary whose first journeys were sponsored by the London Missionary Society but whose later journeys, after he was appointed British consul for the region, were government-sponsored. The region in question was a blank on European maps; Livingstone's travels were the first significant contribution to filling them in, earning him the Gold Medal of the Royal Geographical Society. His missionary work was secondary to his two chief objectives, which were to find the source of the Nile, and to encourage efforts to end the horrendously brutal slave trade run by the Arabs of Zanzibar and Kilwa, preying on the tribes of Central and East Africa. A vignette of what that trade was like is provided by accounts of Livingstone's journey up the Shire River towards Lake Nyasa in December 1862 in his paddle-steamer *Pioneer*; the steamer travelled through regions devastated by slave-hunts, its crew constantly having to clear floating corpses from the steamer's paddle wheels.[4] The two objectives were connected in that Livingstone thought that if he discovered the Nile's source he could use the fame it would bring him as a platform for campaigning against the 'immense evil', as he described it in a letter to a friend, of the trade in human beings.

In Livingstone's view the way to end the slave trade was to bring 'the three Cs' to Africa: 'Christianity, Commerce and Civilisation'. As a missionary he was singularly unsuccessful, converting only one tribal chief. When the Scramble began in the decade after his death, 'Commerce' was the overriding C in Africa itself, but had as much if not more to do with Great Power rivalry back in Europe. 'Christianity' was a mixed blessing given its disruptive effect on tribal customs and relationships.[5] But the effort to end the slave trade was successful, achieved in the decades after Livingstone's death by the hugely increased European presence in Africa; this at least was a positive outcome.

In a Britain – and in a Europe and an America – fed on sensationalist tabloid journalism then as now, the adventures, perils, and discoveries of explorers in Africa were excitedly consumed, bringing the continent's mysteries and possibilities into public consciousness. Before this, Africa was to outside eyes just its coasts – the Barbary Coast, the Windward Coast, the Swahili Coast, and so on, the interior an 'enigmatic blank'[6] – only the accessible West African and South African hinterlands being consciously within the world's purview (North Africa had of course been so for millennia, its history really counting as part of Mediterranean and Near Eastern history). Yet between Livingstone's death and the first years of the twentieth century, a mere three decades, almost the entire continent of Africa came into European possession, sliced like a Christmas cake into colonies and protectorates by six European states. The Scramble prompted nasty and (for Britain) costly and humiliating if eventually successful wars against the Mahdi's followers in the Sudan and Zulus and Boers in South Africa, genocidal atrocities by Germany in South-West Africa, the laying of foundations for a brutal colonial regime in the Congo, and the building of tensions at home in Europe itself that played a significant role in triggering war in 1914.

The belief that there were large opportunities in the African hinterland, markets and resources beckoning to anyone enterprising enough to access them, was enough by itself to encourage exploration and the signing of treaties with tribal chiefs. At first this was done by individual explorers sponsored by private and public bodies at home in Europe. But as the 1880s dawned it was as if a virus of anxiety gripped European governments, suddenly fearing that they might lose their chance of a share of the spoils, prompting a rush to grab as much of Africa as possible. From this point on the Scramble was fully under way.

Some commentators nominate the Berlin Conference of 1884 (also called the 'Congo Conference' and the 'West Africa Conference') as the trigger moment; others more plausibly see the holding of that conference as an acknowledgement of the fact that the Scramble was already in progress, and as aiming to bring some order to the division of the continent among the parties already busily engaged in it.[7] The principal parties were Britain, France, Portugal, Italy, and Germany itself – and King Leopold II of Belgium through his 'International Congo Society'. Spain's geographical relationship with north Africa made it a participant also; it took possession of Equatorial Guinea and brought in Cubans as colonists, while also laying claim to a number of small islands off the Moroccan coast. Other nations participating in the conference – the US, Russia, Denmark, the Netherlands, Austria-Hungary, and the Ottoman Empire – gained no African possessions. One good outcome of the conference was the parties' unanimous commitment to end slavery, which, with the ivory trade, was the chief industry of Arabs and a number of African tribes such as the Yao in the region between the Sahara and the Zambezi. For the Scramble itself, the most significant clause of the conference's concluding General Act was its definition of which regions of the continent lay in the sphere of influence of which of the six chief Scrambling parties.

Several reasons for the Scramble are offered by commentators. One was that the 1870s saw the beginning of a prolonged recession in Europe, the 'Great Depression', triggered by a 'crash' in 1873. It lasted in all European economies into the 1890s, revenues and profits falling steadily throughout the period compared to the mid-century boom years when Britain's neighbours were hastening to emulate its industrial progress. A restraining factor on the French, German, and other European economies was the great lead that the British economy had in out-trading and underselling them around the world. The historian George Sanderson commented that this was so:

> not only in Britain's vast overseas possessions, but in the markets of Latin America, East Asia, and coastal Africa – in fact, wherever free trade prevailed, or could be made to prevail by the guns of British warships. Only in the comparatively limited colonial holdings of other powers could the keen edge of British competition be blunted by discriminatory tariffs and other restrictions. The obvious solution for these powers was to add to their colonial holdings; but after 1815 British naval hegemony was very effectively used (and nowhere more effectively than on the African coasts) to discourage annexations which would create the quasi-monopolistic trading enclaves for other powers.[8]

British naval supremacy created and controlled an 'informal empire' additional to its formal empire, an arrangement that 'safeguarded and even created conditions of free trade which guaranteed Britain's economic preponderance'.[9] Operating an informal empire was strongly regarded by successive British governments as preferable to the expensive and more laborious option of formal colonisation. British policy in Africa up to the time of the Scramble was, accordingly, not to claim territory but to stop others from doing so. For other European powers the opposite policy was preferable, because formal annexation of territory meant that they could exclude British commerce from it and permanently control the acquired market.

It was a British innovation that lent spurs to the other European powers' acquisitive ambitions: the railway. A railway offered dizzying prospects of penetrating the hinterlands of coastal bases to access the rich resources and markets believed to exist there. Chief examples were the French plan to create a Senegal–Niger line and to lay tracks across the Sahara, and Cecil Rhodes' dream of a Cape-to-Cairo railroad as the spine of British Africa. The hinterlands beckoned because the coast-based trade, whose principal points were Zanzibar on the Indian Ocean and the mouths of the Niger and Congo rivers on the Atlantic Ocean, was hostage to conditions in the interior – to African producers and therefore to tribal and inter-tribal politics – and to the fact that supply was controlled by Arab and African middlemen. Tribal conflicts and disruption by slaving raids in the interior made the volumes of supply fluctuate, which made revenue predictions unreliable. Only if river navigation by gunboats was possible could Europeans exert some control on what was happening inland.

Another and in the end more compelling technology was advanced armament: the breech-loading rifle and the Maxim machine gun. Both were of major significance in aiding European suppression of resistance, while the rifle was of not much less significance as an item of trade, and (as gifts) for winning the allegiance of tribal rulers, who coveted guns. Sanderson speculates that the new weapons might have speeded the Scramble, remarking that although advanced weaponry was 'not a necessary condition for the

European partition of Africa' given that 'Frenchmen had already subjugated Algeria, Turco-Egyptians the Sudan, and Afrikaners and Englishmen South Africa, without benefit of *armes perfectionnées* . . . the small-arms revolution may well have not only encouraged, but accelerated, the scramble – especially by sometimes enabling quite small European expeditions to plant flags and extort "treaties" deep in the African interior.'[10]

A major reason explorers had for exaggerating the copiousness of resources and the size of potential markets in the continent's interior was their interest in securing funding for further expeditions. It was the fantasies this prompted, of 'totally mythical El Dorados . . . of vast, fertile, empty lands, African "Sleeping Beauties" awaiting the magic kiss of European energy, skill and capital; or, in bewildering contradiction, manufacturers' El Dorados of millions of eager potential customers', that led enough members of European governments to see Africa as the solution to the problem of persistent economic recession at home.[11] Thus was hope of profit the touch-paper for the Scramble. For as soon as one European power made a hope-inspired grab at a piece of Africa, the rest felt compelled to do likewise – or, in Britain's case, to act in order to pre-empt efforts by others to do so.

For most of the nineteenth century Britain had been successful in limiting French attempts to increase its holdings in North Africa and to gain larger footholds in West and East Africa, most of both of them lying within Britain's 'informal empire'. Until the 1880s France was almost alone in trying to loosen the British grip. Portuguese attempts to establish posts on both sides of the Congo River mouth had been peremptorily prevented by London, illustrating the weakness of any putative partners to French efforts. France, partly because of its determination to restore its position as a major European power after defeat by Prussia in 1870, and partly because of inflammation of its traditional rivalry with Britain caused by the latter's assertion of unilateral control over Egypt,[12] increased its desire to create a great empire in west and north Africa, intending eventually to embrace as much of the continent as lay between its possessions of Senegal and Algeria. This was a matter, therefore, of prestige as well as economics; and it was prestige also that figured in Bismarck's sudden desire to make the newly created German Empire a player in Africa, announcing annexations of South-West Africa (now Namibia) and 'German East Africa' (now Tanzania).[13]

While Italy was appropriating Eritrea, Somalia, and Ethiopia and merging them as its Italian East Africa colony, the biggest single tranche of sub-Saharan Africa – indeed, an enormous tranche of the heart of the continent – was being taken not by a state but by a person: King Leopold II of the Belgians, who with adroitness and subtlety – not to say subterfuge – had, against the wishes of his own government and under the noses of the other scrambling powers, taken the immensity of the Congo with its jungles and mighty river as his own personal fiefdom. The intricate story of how he managed it is told by Thomas Pakenham in *The Scramble for Africa*.[14] In all these cases some antecedent claim, or pretext, was invoked in justification for a grab; Leopold's agent in the Congo region was the American-British adventurer-journalist Henry Stanley of 'Dr Livingstone I presume' fame; in East Africa it was a German explorer, Johannes Rebmann, who first saw Mount Kilimanjaro, thus giving Germany its excuse; while for France it was (Italian-born) Pierre de Brazza who served its interests in French Equatorial Africa ('Congo Brazzaville').

The British had many such claims. They included the push north from South Africa sponsored by Cecil Rhodes, Livingstone's extensive travels from coast to coast in the region between the Zambezi River and the great lakes, and the British annexation of the Sultan of Zanzibar's domains (over which it had already long exerted *de facto* control). These resulted in the territories first known as British Central Africa (Bechuanaland, the Rhodesias, and Nyasaland) and British East Africa (Kenya, Uganda, and eventually Tanganyika). Add Egypt, the Sudan, and British Somaliland (with Aden across the water from the Horn of Africa), with in the west Nigeria, Sierra Leone, Gambia, and the Gold Coast, and one sees how extensive Britain's possessions were. France could claim the biggest single country in Africa – Algeria – and Italy the oldest Christian civilisation in Africa – Ethiopia – while the Portuguese, with their possessions on the west and east coasts (Angola and Mozambique respectively), could claim to have been first to navigate along Africa's coasts. But none compared with the sheer extent of Britain's holdings in all quarters of the African compass.

Given that some of Britain's control of these territories was, until the Scramble, supposedly indirect, employing the 'informal empire' technique of governing through putative local rulers as in Egypt and Zanzibar – a model perfected in the princely states of India – the fact that it was galvanised into formal annexations, either as colonies or protectorates, with acceptance of the expense of doing so, is a mark of Scramble pressure. That pressure was exerted through the politics of Europe. For a prime example: French annoyance with what the British had done in pushing it out of partnership in Egypt resulted in a temporary Franco–German alignment which allowed Germany to take parts of Britain's informal empire in South-West and East Africa. (Germany did not hold them long; after its defeat in 1918 the first was placed under South African control by a League of Nations mandate – and thus effectively back into Britain's informal empire – while the second was annexed outright by Britain.)

As this shows, a significant aspect of the Scramble was the seeking of diplomatic advantage in Europe itself. The movement of men and arms in Africa was the shadow of policy moves in the chancelleries of Europe. For example: Britain's advance into the Sudan in 1896 was not revenge for General Gordon's defeat and death at Khartoum in 1885 at the hands of the Mahdi,[15] but was a gesture of goodwill to Italy, which asked for help because the Mahdists were preparing to attack Eritrea. Italy had been defeated by Menelik of Ethiopia at the Battle of Adowa (Adwa) in March 1896, and the Mahdists were seeking to profit from Italian weakness. Italy was allied to Germany and Austria-Hungary – the Triple Alliance – and because the alliance's leader Germany was keen to keep ties between Britain and France weak, and at the same time wished to test Britain's preparedness to be on good terms with itself, it seconded Italy's request for British aid. Berlin 'saw in London's response to Italy a crucial test of the entire orientation of British foreign policy, which was in effect being constrained to "choose" between France and Germany'.[16] The British accordingly sent a token force into the Sudan as a diplomatic gesture; within two years the expedition had mushroomed into a major war, of which the centrepiece was the Battle of Omdurman, bringing Sudan wholly under British control. As an illustration of the effect on Africa of European diplomatic manoeuvring, nothing could be more stark.

Some histories of the Scramble suggest that 'the Flag followed the Gospel', giving missionary activity a significant role in the colonisation process, annexation following conversion. This is acknowledged to be so in Nyasaland, catechised by Presbyterians; but chiefly because the British Prime Minister in office at the time, Lord Salisbury, knowing that the only route into Nyasaland was through Portugal's Mozambique, was unwilling to see Scottish Presbyterian votes lost as a result of Portuguese Catholics claiming the territory if Britain neglected to do so. Elsewhere the missionaries of one country found themselves preaching and praying under flags not their own – French White Fathers under the Union Jack in Uganda, British Baptists variously under France's Tricolour or Germany's black, white, and red.

In analysing the reasons for the Scramble – among them hopes of economic advantage, diplomatic imperatives in Europe, and the general ripening of imperial possibilities through exploration and missionary activity – two not so far mentioned are of equal if not greater importance. One is what Sanderson calls 'the breakdown of informal empire'.[17] The other is complicity and involvement by Africans themselves in the colonising process, a product of Africa's own internal politics, a process Richard Reid calls the 'co-option of Europe' into Africa's own patterns and dynamics of change.[18] As Reid shows, Africans were not wholly passive victims of European expropriation everywhere in the continent, but sometimes used, or allied with, European activity for ends and needs of their own.

It is, however, the first of these factors, 'the breakdown of informal empire', added to those of profit, national prestige, and current diplomatic practicalities, that is relevant to thinking about what might happen in space.

On the eve of the Scramble, Britain was the paramount power in Africa. Indeed 'paramountcy' was a concept developed by British policy-makers to give the idea of informal empire a more – paradoxical as it seems – formal cast, so that other governments would know where not to trespass. 'In the many regions where Britain exercised exclusive influence without having acquired formal possession she was increasingly ready to claim, as "paramount power", a quasi-legal right of objection to any encroachment by other powers'.[19] Until the late 1870s this claim was not contested by anyone, though part of the French government, the

Colonial Office, was eager to do so, having to be restrained by the French Foreign Office – always known by the name of its location, the Quai d'Orsay – because of France's tenuous diplomatic position following the Franco–Prussian War and its sequel of tensions over Alsace-Lorraine. But by the late 1870s France's diplomatic position had improved, and in Germany Bismarck was keen to secure the new Reich's interests by promoting rivalry between Britain and France – hence the already-mentioned temporary Franco–German rapprochement enabling the latter to make its own Scramble grabs in Africa.

It was this change in the diplomatic weather that forced Britain's hand in the matter of informal empire and its doctrine of 'paramountcy'. These *de facto* but not *de jure* supports for its claims were no longer sufficient, unless it was prepared to go to actual war to enforce them. It was instead obliged to formalise its claims in response to other Scramblers making formal claims of their own, claims based on justifications in no way legally weaker than Britain's. Thus from the French point of view 'it was now no longer necessary deliberately to sacrifice all colonial opportunity in Africa for the sake of European security, nor to be so strict in restraining the colonial activists; and in November 1880 the Quai d'Orsay issued a directive to this effect.'[20]

Taking all these factors into account, it is not hard to envisage Scramble parallels for a twenty-first-century expansion of human activity into space. The paramount power at time of writing is the US, with an aggressively up-and-coming rival in China. There is nothing new, in terms of terrestrial diplomacy, in techniques of distracting and dividing; China does it in pursuing its irredentist ambitions with respect to the South China Seas and Taiwan, maintains its hold on its land empire in Tibet and Xinjiang, befriends international pariah states such as Russia and Myanmar, and uses its financial and technological advantages to establish an informal empire in Africa, all in time-honoured ways. For its part the US runs its informal empire in almost exactly the same way Britain did it in the nineteenth century, by the almost exact equivalent of the gunboat: to look at a map of US military bases and alliances in Europe and the Pacific Ocean is to see a thick ring of steel around perceived enemies or at least rivals, Russia in the one case and China in the other.

Without venturing into science fiction, any number of analogous lunar scenarios can be described that would inflame terrestrial tensions. Suppose that scientific activities by X identified resources and that Y then proceeded to extract them, excluding X from participation. Suppose that X and Y attempted simultaneously to establish operations in the same locale on the moon, arriving and setting up there at the same time. Suppose a commercial operator from X interfered with the activities of a Y state or commercial operator, even going so far as to damage or destroy Y's equipment when its base was temporarily unmanned (recall the Chilean and Argentinian lighthouses of Snipe Island). Suppose a price war was begun by state X or commercial operators based in X to undercut Y or Y-operators; and suppose that X's resources are greater than Y's, so that its greater economic muscle harmed Y's objectives and interests. Suppose X controls most of the market for consumption of some resource extracted on the moon – hydrogen for rocket fuel, say – with X's presence in space activity far outweighing that of any competitor, thus placing X in *de facto* control of all Y's activities in space. Suppose versions of space piracy occur, commercial operators prompted to it by the *terra nullius* conditions in space and the immense difficulties of policing and enforcing Earth-made agreements; for this possibility an instructive antecedent is the activity of sixteenth-century English privateers raiding the galleons of the Spanish Main, unofficially encouraged by their government at home in London – a fruitful *casus belli.*

No doubt novelists of the appropriate genre will conceive of yet more scenarios. But these are sufficient to indicate why any X which itself, or through its commercial operators, engages in the high-cost and high-reward exploitation of lunar and Martian resources, will take all means necessary to ensure the security of those operations and the personnel engaged in them. Yet further: national advantage, national prestige, and the jockeying web of diplomatic ties on Earth that enhance or protect both, will reprise what happened in the Scramble for Africa, as surely as night follows day. For the international order – to repeat, because this is an essential point – is an anarchy of self-interests only tenuously constrained by expediencies, these latter as shifting as the sparkles of sunlight on the sea; and throughout history the collapse of the arrangements – treaties, agreements, truces, alliances – which mediate those tenuous constraints constitutes history's principal theme: the theme of competition and conflict.

The question that presses, therefore, is this: is the 1967 Outer Space Treaty and its associated agreements good enough to prevent history's principal theme from continuing beyond the limits of Earth's atmosphere, and rebounding into conflicts on Earth itself?

# 5

# IS THE OUTER SPACE TREATY GOOD ENOUGH?

A highly commendable feature of United Nations' attempts to achieve global agreement on globally important matters is the insistence, iterated in all its relevant Resolutions, Declarations, Treaties, and Conventions, on peace and shared benefit. The 1967 Outer Space Treaty – its formal title is 'Treaty on Principles Governing the Activities of States in the Exploration and Use of Outer Space, including the Moon and Other Celestial Bodies' (hereafter 'the Treaty' or, if differentiation from other treaties is required, 'the 1967 Treaty') – begins with an acknowledgement of an 'irreversible fact', and a statement of two aspirations. The irreversible fact is that humanity has 'entered outer space', and the aspirations are that the 'common interest of all mankind' will be recognised and served by *peaceful* exploration and use of this new domain '*for the benefit of all peoples* irrespective of the degree of their economic or scientific development', and that the result will be a strengthening of friendly relations between states and peoples.

The phrase 'the peaceful exploration and use of outer space' or its close variants recurs a number of times throughout the Treaty, the whole tenor of which is directed at serving that aspiration. Nuclear weapons and weapons of mass destruction are banned, and so is assertion of sovereignty by any state over any region either of space or of a celestial body.

But aspirations are just that: aspirations. UN statements of aspirations are made in full knowledge that the attempt to give them effect in the form of international treaties and binding international law carries no guarantee that they will be realised. Resistance to the UNCLOS by the US and other countries is a prime example of the tenuous nature of efforts at international unity of purpose; the US resiling from the 2012 Paris climate accords under Donald Trump's presidency is another. The high barriers of national self-interest and economic imperatives (including, not least among them, the profit motive) are high indeed. This fact is not a reason for abandoning the aspirations in question and giving up attempts to realise them; indeed the aspirations, by themselves alone, are not without effect in restraining behaviour and – even more so – in shaping attitudes in positive ways. But as with all treaties, they depend on achieving sufficiently worthwhile agreement and on signatory parties adhering to the agreement thereafter. Achieving agreement can be difficult and often happens courtesy of compromises that undermine some aspect of the desired effectiveness, while the risk of parties failing to comply or withdrawing wholly is the great weakness of any international treaty because that is the permanent threat they face.

The principal and familiar reason why states might be reluctant to agree to, or to comply fully with, or to remain permanently bound by, agreements is national self-interest. This in turn is a complex consisting of determination not to fall behind in competitive advantage economically, together with considerations of national prestige, history, and existing alliances and enmities in relation to other states. These motivations outweigh logic, which dictates that if commons such as the bed of the high seas and outer space are to be used for commercial benefit, then the benefit should be as common – in the sense of 'as shared' – as the common itself. That is what the UN treaties seek to achieve. Small players are considerably more amenable to the concept of sharing than are big players, a phenomenon as familiar in the school playground as it was to Thucydides' Athenians when they reminded the people of the little but recalcitrant island state of Melos that 'the right, as the world goes, is only in question between equal powers; otherwise the strong do what they can and the weak suffer what they must'.[1] The US's refusal to be party to UNCLOS is a paradigmatic example of why international agreement is so hard to achieve and sustain.

It was not, however, difficult for the UN to get agreement to and ratification of the 1967 Outer Space Treaty. The circumstances in which it was adopted made it easy: it is a Cold War treaty, and its principal drivers were the US and the USSR engaged in the self-inflaming complex of a space race, an arms race, and a tense military stand-off. To park outer space – like parking the Antarctic – somewhere geopolitically innocuous was of advantage to both sides; hence the relative ease with which agreement was attained. The difficult part is its sustainability.

The reason why the Treaty will be difficult to sustain is that for all the excellence of its intentions, it is inadequate to the unfolding situation in space both as regards commercial exploitation of resources there by private enterprise, and as regards its rapid militarisation. The Treaty creates no mechanism other than itself – in the form of the aspirations it expresses – to prevent conflict in space, to intervene if it occurs, to adjudicate between conflicting parties, and to ensure that the outcomes of adjudications are observed. The Treaty states that international law is as applicable in outer space as it is terrestrially (Articles I and III), but it does not give effect to it in space by means of a body or authority (as UNCLOS attempts to do with regard to the deep seabed), instead requiring individual states to administer the law to themselves and to entities operating from within them (Article VI). By the same token, it puts nothing in place to ensure that the benefits from exploitation of resources in space – chiefly, commercial profit – will be shared 'for the benefit of all peoples'. And it has not stopped the militarisation of space; the ban on nuclear weapons and weapons of mass destruction in the Treaty's Preamble and Article IV does not cover conventional weapons and weapons (such as lasers and cyber-attack technologies) that did not exist, or did not exist in their current form, in 1967, and it is precisely these that are now variously filling or targeting the orbital zones around Earth, and will as easily come to operate on the moon, among asteroids and – soon enough – on Mars.

To understand these points better one has to look at context, involving three matters: how the Treaty came into existence, the nature of commercial prospects and activities in space, and what is happening in the militarisation of space alongside these latter developments.

Although penetration of the aerial spaces above human heads first happened long ago – in the form of tall buildings such as pyramids, ziggurats, and towers (the tower unearthed archaeologically within the walls of Jericho is dated to 8000 BCE), followed after about nine millennia by Chinese-invented rockets for warfare and entertainment (believed to have originated in the Sung Dynasty 960–1279 CE), followed by hot-air balloons in the eighteenth century – it was not until the first decade of the twentieth century that thoughts of a need for a 'Law of Space' were mooted. The prompt was realisation that heavier-than-air flight, and radio transmission, raises questions about whether the airspaces above states are commons like the high seas, or are national territory; and if the latter, how far up into the air national sovereignty extends.

It was a Belgian lawyer, Emile Laude, who asked this question in connection with radio waves, since these travel through the sky above all and any national territory. He observed that 'the problem of the ownership and use' of radio waves (he called them 'Hertzian waves') would one day prompt the need for a 'Law of Space'.[2] In the years after the First World War the more practical matter of sovereignty over the altitudes accessible to aircraft was a focus of international debate; at a conference on the question in Moscow in 1926 it was taken as read that states have 'complete sovereignty' over their airspace, though the question of 'defining the altitude at which the international zone begins' above that airspace was, as the senior Soviet official V. A. Zarzar noted, left unresolved.[3] As this shows, it was already recognised that a distinction is needed between airspace and outer space, and the first thorough examination of the implications of that distinction was made by the remarkable lawyer and inventor Dr Vladimir Mandl in a short monograph published in 1932.[4]

Mandl was both interested in and prescient about the development of rocketry (he himself patented a design for a high-altitude rocket). He saw that a legal regime for space had to be different from both airspace and maritime law, asserting that beyond territorial airspace 'there begins an area which has no relation to our globe and therefore to any individual part of the Earth's surface, which is no longer Earth appurtenant and is therefore free of any terrestrial State power, *coelum liberum*. In this area, the traffic of spaceships is completely free.'[5] The reference to Grotius' concept of *mare liberum* is direct, and Mandl's iteration of it underlies the UN's Resolution 1721 of 1961 stating that 'Outer space and celestial bodies are free for exploration and use by all States in conformity with international law and are not subject to national appropriation.'[6]

It is easy to make airy and even idealistic generalisations about subject-matters which are in no danger of being imminent realities, but Mandl saw that space was indeed coming within human reach, and with much insight discussed 'the nationality of spaceships, the construction of ports in outer space, economic exploration of space resources, [and] effects of space activities on culture'.[7] The one topic on which his prescience fell short was the militarisation of space, stating his belief that 'spaceships for a time of war' would only be 'auxiliary means to the land, sea or air forces without forming an independent weapon system'.[8]

One of the most striking thoughts in Mandl's book concerns the possibility that as humanity colonises space, the connection with terrestrial nationality will become questionable, with space-based individuals entering into new communities eventually detached from national affiliations on Earth. The implication Mandl saw was that, in such a circumstance, 'no earthly State will be in a position to exercise an organized control over another celestial body in order to bring into effect its laws there', with the consequence that 'legal control will thus be illusory and indeed, not only in that distant region but also on Earth itself'.[9] In other words one has to acknowledge that the prospect is no longer merely fanciful that, in a further future, communities established on the moon or elsewhere in the solar system might become independent of Earth, reprising the history of colonisation and decolonisation on Earth itself, and even that competition and conflict might arise between or among them. This possibility is the greater when private actors are the colonisers and exploiters of new domains.

Soon after Mandl's book was published, a Soviet legal expert, Yevgeny Korovin, addressed the question of 'conquest of the stratosphere' by hot-air balloons that could be used for aerial bombing, smuggling, surveillance, or reconnaissance by optical and infrared means, and other harms to subjacent people and property.[10] In this respect Korovin was more prescient than Mandl about the negative, and in particular military, implications of the penetration of space. He argued that the principle of sovereignty over airspace accessible to airplanes must be extended to include any superjacent space above a national territory, speed and altitude making no difference to the legal status of any form of overflight. He accordingly argued that a state had the right to defend the space over their national territory by any means they saw fit. The impracticality of his view was summarised in an article by the physicist and science fiction writer Arthur C. Clarke of *2001: A Space Odyssey* fame, who pointed out that as Earth rotated every country would be claiming sovereignty over every region of space.[11]

Korovin's dissent from the view that Zarzar and Mandl had stressed, namely that there is an absolute difference between airspace and outer space from the legal as well as the technical point of view, proved ineffective; it was the latter view that prevailed. It is curious that the implicit analogy between the high seas and space failed to take into account that the former had so often been the scene of warfare and piracy, the latter indeed potentiated by the lack of any jurisdiction over them; in this respect Korovin had anticipated possibilities that Mandl and others had not. And at that time the extent of overfishing of Earth's oceans was not appreciated, so that the likelihood of a tragedy of the commons occurring in space was not even considered.

The imminence and then actuality of world war in the 1930s and 1940s both galvanised and hid the developments in rocket science that, had their extent been fully appreciated, might have changed or at least supplemented views like Mandl's that space presented no military threat, though by the war's end it was clear that humanity's reach into space was already a likelihood. And indeed it was not much more than a decade after the end of hostilities that the first satellites were placed in orbit, during the International Geophysical Year of 1957. In the years leading to that point – and that point was the trigger for the space race that ensued between the US and the USSR – it became clear that an upper limit to national sovereignty over airspace had to be established so that the legal status of space operations was itself clear. At the same time there were expressions of concern about the technically advanced nations laying claim to regions of space or celestial bodies as had happened on Earth in the age of colonisation, and in various discussions the phrase 'the common heritage of mankind' began to appear in relation to the moon and the solar system.[12] In the 1950s therefore 'the flood gates were opened, and space law articles and papers began to appear with increasing frequency', notable names among contributors to the debate being Alex Meyer of the University of Cologne, John Cobb Cooper of McGill University in Canada, Welf Heinrich Prince of Hanover, and Joseph Kroell.[13]

Meyer expressed concern about the militarisation of space, arguing that military operations should be expressly forbidden there. In the event, when the 1967 Treaty was formulated the major anxiety was the placement of nuclear weapons and weapons of mass destruction in space, and conventional weapons – then-current weapons technology being such that they did not figure very largely in treaty-makers' deliberations – were left out of account. Instead, the debate among space law theoreticians focused on such matters as radio frequency requirements and regulation, given their essential role in space flight. This reflected the fact that officials of the US, Soviet, and other governments were now fully in the debate, as was the International Congress on Astronautics, which in 1957 established a specialist standing committee on legal questions relating to space, and through it communicated to the UN its hope that international agreement could be reached on the matter. The observation that space was a legal vacuum, and that earlier agreements about airspace sovereignty and regulation (such as the important Chicago Convention of 1944 governing airplane traffic around the globe) did not apply to space, made an overwhelming case for a concerted international effort to settle the matter.

In response to this growing debate, and in light of two alarming developments – the rapid technological developments in the space race triggered by the launch of Sputnik I in 1957, and the heating up of the Cold War (eventually precipitating near-disaster in the Cuban missile crisis of October 1962) – the UN General Assembly established a Committee on the Peaceful Uses of Outer Space in 1959 and work began on proposals for a treaty. In 1961 the General Assembly adopted Resolutions 1721 and 1802, both entitled 'International Cooperation in the Peaceful Uses of Outer Space', and in 1963 adopted Resolution 1962, entitled

'Declaration of Legal Principles Governing the Activities of States in the Exploration and Use of Outer Space', containing all the elements of the eventual 1967 Treaty. These were passed unanimously.

With the addition to the Treaty of agreements about rescuing astronauts in distress (1968), liability for damage caused by space-related activity (1972), and registration of objects launched into space (1975), the Treaty system went as far as it could until hitting a barrier: its failure to gather support for an 'Agreement Governing the Activities of States on the Moon and Other Celestial Bodies', which opened for signature in 1979 and, although technically coming into force in 1984 upon receiving its fifth signature, has never come near attracting a sufficient number of signatures to be effective.

The failure of the 1979 agreement attempt is highly significant. Its preamble states, '*Determined* to promote on the basis of equality the further development of cooperation among States in the exploration and use of the Moon and celestial bodies, *Desiring* to prevent the Moon from becoming an area of international conflict . . . *Taking into account* the need to define and develop the provisions of [the 1967 Treaty and associated agreements] in relation to the Moon and other celestial bodies, [and] having regard to further progress in the exploration and use of outer space'. This amounts to recognition that the 1967 Treaty required clarification and updating with particular reference to the moon, a fact that the lapse of four decades since then has only made more urgent, a point reinforced by Artemis (see below) and other moon exploration and commercial development programmes.

The failed 1979 effort made the UN hesitant to seek new formal treaties, so it resorted instead to the less ambitious expedient of non-binding Resolutions in an effort to guide space activity into paths exclusively peaceful and productive. A number of problems were addressed in this tentative manner, chief among them the overlapping of satellite broadcast signals, with its potential for deliberate interference in the 'free flow of information' (a characteristic UN aspiration for the world), remote sensing including surveillance of other states' infrastructure and military, and the question of nuclear power sources on spacecraft. But even these efforts were less persuasive than the earlier consensus on space; with the effective end of the Cold War in 1989 the US, as the single remaining superpower, 'felt more and more inclined to lose an interest in concerted UN space law-making'.[14]

The increasingly rapid rate of technological change in the decade after the Cold War's end even further outpaced the UN's regime of agreements about space. Chief among the developments was the internet. What had started in 1969 as an initiative of the US Department of Defence to enable different government and university computers to exchange data became, by the early 1990s, the internet, as increasingly many commercial operators linked into the network. So quickly did the data demands of the internet grow that by the end of the 1990s operators began to look not merely to geostationary satellites but to networked constellations of them to provide the larger and faster capacity for internet traffic than the earthbound 'packet-switching' architecture allowed. That development duly took place; by the 2020s the crowded orbital zones around Earth were replete with constellations of networked satellites, the largest of them at time of writing being Starlink operated by SpaceX. Others include Globalstar, OneWeb, Iridium, Inmarsat, and Thuraya.

These developments introduced a different perspective from the point of view of law: the perspective of space as a cyber as well as a physical domain, one which is no longer straightforwardly amenable to governance by state-monopoly means, but with a large number of non-state actors and agencies at work, posing problems of security, of competition and conflict over spectrum allocations, and of both physical and electromagnetic threats to the reliability of operations.[15]

The physical 'space trash' problem is that Low Earth Orbit, where satellite constellations fly – an already 'crowded and congested' zone – has become littered with debris from collisions, rocket fragments, dead satellites which have failed to obey instructions to move to 'graveyard' orbits or to return for burn-up in the atmosphere, and the thousands of still-circulating pieces left over from a Chinese anti-satellite (ASAT) weapon test which blew up a retired Chinese satellite in 2007.

The electromagnetic threats take the form of malicious hacking, described by Jason Fritz in 2013 as falling into four main types: jamming, eavesdropping, hijacking, and controlling.[16] In the opinion of Larry Martinez of California State University, the changed realities of space require a move away from the 'hard law', top-down model exemplified by state-monopoly governance as in the 1967 Treaty, to a 'soft law' model – a 'collaborative commons model' – in which an 'open access structure for the multi-stakeholder Internet community' makes space a more sustainable domain through voluntary agreements on such matters as debris and hacking.[17]

These thoughts have much to recommend them in relation to space as cyberspace, but the more old-fashioned physical facts of extraction operations on the moon and the establishment of permanent or reusable bases there – and eventually of both on Mars – seem to fall under the conventional rubric of what the 1967 Treaty addresses. The new cyber realities were not then fully conceived, a hole in the Treaty that most certainly needs filling. Physical occupation and resource extraction were indeed anticipated, and one important question is whether the Treaty is still adequate to them. The challenge facing the international community in deciding how to manage what happens on the moon and elsewhere in the local regions of the solar system has, accordingly, grown.

A sceptic might respond to the foregoing points by saying that commercial activity on the moon and Mars is going to be so limited because of practical difficulties and cost that anxieties about legal and military complications are excessive – they can be dealt with, the sceptic might say, on a piecemeal basis if and when they arise, which will not be often; the broad statement of principles in the Treaty and subsequent agreements is good enough. Given the considerations of expense and engineering challenges that have seen various space programmes scrapped or delayed in the first decades of the twenty-first century (including NASA's Constellation Program 2005–9 and the Asteroid Redirect Mission, 'ARM', proposed in 2013), the sceptic's argument would appear to have force – supplemented, as it is, by the failure (at time of writing) of most efforts by private companies to achieve successful lunar landings. The first private company to try, Japan's ispace, launched its Hakuto-R M1 lunar lander from Cape Canaveral, Florida, on a SpaceX Falcon 9 rocket in December 2022, aiming to land in the Atlas Crater at the edge of Mare Frigoris in the moon's northern hemisphere. The module carried two rovers, one made by the Japanese space agency JAXA, designed to test requirements for a future manned lunar rover, the other – named Rashid – a surface-exploration rover funded by the Mohammed Bin Rashid Space Centre of the United Arab Emirates.[18] All went well until M1 descended to the lunar surface on Tuesday 25 April 2023, at which point it fell silent, an ispace spokesman saying that it had most likely crashed on landing.

M1's loss joined four other space failures in the early months of 2023 – SpaceX, JAXA, ABL Space Systems, and Relativity Space all lost rockets to technical problems. But there were positives also; SpaceX's Falcon 9 rockets had already proved consistently reliable, and had successfully taken M1 to its lunar rendezvous, with no responsibility for what subsequently happened in the module landing phase. The European Space Agency successfully launched its Jupiter probe 'Juice' ('Jupiter Icy Moons Explorer') in the same month that M1 failed, a part of the continuing and developing exploration of the solar system which will eventually take human beings and their activities beyond the moon. Add to these India's lunar successes.

Despite all the setbacks for private enterprise's first-ever lunar efforts, the sceptic's argument has, therefore, already been refuted by events. A spokesperson for ispace said that much had been learned from the M1 effort and that M2 was already being built. Even as the M1 failure occurred, five other lunar landing projects were underway for 2023, two of them by private companies, Intuitive Machines of Houston and Astrobotic Technology of Pittsburgh. The former partnered with SpaceX to place a lander on the moon's south pole; the latter chose to have its lander, aiming for the Ocean of Storms, launched on a Vulcan Centaur rocket. Three government space programmes also planned lunar landings in the course of the year: India's Chandrayaan-3, Japan's SLIM ('Smart Lander for Investigating Moon'), and Russia's space agency Roscosmos' Luna-25 mission. The fact that several of these missions were delayed from previous years because of technical problems is an indication not of the tenuousness of lunar landing efforts, but of the determination to make them succeed: and it is this fact – the scale of activity already reached at time of writing, its persistence and continual accumulation of expertise and experience – that makes the exploitation of lunar resources and eventual settlement of the moon inevitable, for each increment of such activity has a multiplier effect, generating yet more activity.

Note the designation of the Roscosmos mission: 'Luna-25'. Luna-24 was a lunar surface sample mission flown in 1976. Nearly half a century later, and in the midst of a highly self-damaging war, Russia's resolve to return to the moon indicates its anxiety about falling behind in the increasing space activity by so many players. Not least among these is China, in whose Chang'e series of lunar landings the latest (at time of writing) collected and returned to Earth samples of the moon's surface; this was Chang'e 5, launched in November 2020 and landing successfully near Mons Rümker, returning to Earth with two kilograms of lunar soil a month later.[19] Chang'e missions 6, 7, and 8, scheduled for 2025, 2026, and 2028 respectively, are intended to pave the way for manned flight to the moon in the 2030s and the establishment of a base, the 'International Lunar Research Station', at the moon's south pole. The 'international' in the name marks that the project is a partnership with Russia, announced in 2021, and the two countries issued an invitation to other countries to join them in it, forming an International Lunar Research Station Cooperation Organization (ILRSCO).

'Where you might just see gray rocks, soil and craters on the moon, entrepreneurs see profit':[20] publicly sponsored space efforts are accordingly leveraging the profit motive to work with private enterprise. NASA set up its Commercial Lunar Payload Services programme to this end, following the success of its use of private companies for travelling to and from the International Space Station. CLPS is a component of the Artemis programme (named after the Greek goddess of the moon) founded in 2017 by NASA in conjunction with the European Space Agency, the Canadian Space Agency, and Japan's JAXA.

Artemis was boosted by the US Congress's passage of its Commercial Space Launch Competitiveness Act of 2015 stating that US citizens can legally recover resources in space.

Both Russia and China opposed this concept in public fora. The resulting Artemis Accords have been signed by over twenty countries. They iterate the 1967 Treaty's principles of peaceful cooperation for the use of the moon, Mars, and asteroids, and take full advantage of the Treaty's encouragement of exploration and resource exploitation. In accordance with the latter, in particular, NASA has nominated more than a dozen private companies to make scientific instruments and to transport them and other cargo to the moon as part of CLPS. At time of writing there are approximately a dozen moon landers in production by commercial companies in the US. The incentive for Artemis's private partners includes the prospect of mining platinum and rare earths, processing ice water for rocket fuel, and using the moon or moon-orbiting stations as launch pads for access to Mars, asteroids, comets, and the solar system in general.[21]

Artemis 1 launched in 2022 with robots and mannequins aboard, testing its Space Launch System and the Orion spacecraft that on subsequent missions 2 to 5 will carry human crew. The mission was successful. The rest of the programme is ambitious, designed to put a 'Lunar Gateway' space station in orbit around the moon and human feet back on the moon's surface in 2025, with eventual building of a permanent base there as a waystation for human-crewed missions to Mars.

Artemis arose from the rubble of several previously abandoned projects, chiefly the Constellation project initiated under President George W. Bush's presidency in 2005. The Orion spacecraft intended for Constellation was kept alive under President Obama's 2010 NASA Authorization Act, and with it development of the Space Launch System and plans for three programmes key to commercial space activity: the Commercial Crew Development programme, the Commercial Resupply Services, and the Commercial Orbital Transportation Services.[22] The official website of the Artemis programme begins with an eye-catching announcement: 'With Artemis missions, NASA will land the first woman and first person of color on the Moon, using innovative technologies to explore more of the lunar surface than ever before. We will collaborate with commercial and international partners and establish the first long-term presence on the Moon. Then, we will use what we learn on and around the Moon to take the next giant leap: sending the first astronauts to Mars.'[23]

The Sino-Russian ILRSCO is intentionally a rival to Artemis. Whereas the latter stresses collaboration with 'commercial partners', it is not clear to what extent the former will do likewise; no doubt the nature of international partners will be an influence in that matter. Equally without doubt, the involvement of commercial interests in Artemis is motivated by financial even more than ideological grounds; the sheer ambition of the project over the long term would be a major burden on taxpayers in the participating countries if that was the sole source of funding, as had been the case in the first phase of lunar missions. But whether or not private enterprise comes to play a significant role in ILRSCO, the presence of commercial players in the Artemis endeavour, and the presence of commercial players independently of Artemis who would expect the space version of consular support by their home states, complicates further the potential for rivalry in what is in effect a reprise of the twentieth century's West–East binary. This is because private enterprise in space introduces a potential for 'loose cannon' events, off-piste activity, and non-conformity with such norms and standards as are taken to be implied by the spirit at least (where explicit text is absent) of the 1967 Treaty and associated UN instruments and resolutions.

This would be a cause for concern in its own right even if the militarisation of space were not happening more rapidly than commercial and civil developments. The medium- and long-term implications of their coincidence are grave.

The militarisation of space began, in fact, with the space age itself; within the first fifteen years following the launch of the world's first artificial satellite, Sputnik I, both the US and USSR had surveillance satellites in orbit, and were developing anti-satellite technologies ranging from 'directed-energy weapons' (lasers, particle beams, microwaves, sound beams) to ASAT missiles and kamikaze satellites. Part of the flight paths of intercontinental ballistic missiles (ICBMs) lies in space, and accordingly defence systems involve placement in space or targeting out into space. The US tried a number of systems – countering nuclear warheaded ICBMs with nuclear warheaded ICBMs over the North Pole (this was the 1950s Nike-Zeus proposal), in the 1960s Project Defender which sought to target Soviet launch sites from armed satellites in orbit, and after that the Sentinel and Safeguard systems with dedicated anti-ICBM missiles (ABMs). Then in the 1980s under President Ronald Reagan the Strategic Defense Initiative (SDI, colloquially known as 'Star Wars') proposed placing anti-missile defences in orbit. There is wide agreement that the initiative was a significant factor in the ending of the Cold War and the collapse of the USSR because the expense of countering the SDI was beyond Moscow's capacity.

While the SDI was on the table in the mid-1980s the US formed its Space Command (USSPACECOM) as part of the United States Air Force. The 1991 Gulf War – the US-led alliance's expulsion of invading Iraqi forces from Kuwait – is described as the world's 'first space war' because of the vital role played by satellites in command and control communications, targeting, and surveillance. From then on satellite systems have been integral to military activity in all areas of conflict. The rapidly growing importance of space-based technologies for military activity led to the evolution of USSPACECOM into the United States Space Force, established in 2019, as an independent arm of the US military, whose chief sits on the Joint Chiefs of Staff Committee. It is the world's first independent space army.

Critics of the formation of the US Space Force remarked on its rhetoric and the cosmetics of its uniform and badging; members of the Force are known as 'Guardians' and their appearance is sufficiently reminiscent of Marvel comic-book heroes to elicit comment. The published space-war doctrine of the Force opens with the statement:

> United States Space Force (USSF) doctrine guides the proper use of military spacepower in support of the Service's cornerstone responsibilities. It establishes a common frame of reference on the best way to plan and employ Space Force forces as

> part of a broader joint force. This doctrine provides official advice and describes the parameters to execute and leverage spacepower utilizing its core competencies. It is not directive – rather, it provides Guardians an informed starting point for decision making and mission execution.[24]

Both the Russian and Chinese space forces are incorporated into their existing military structures. Russia's Space Force is one of the three primary branches of its Aerospace Forces, while China's People's Liberation Army Strategic Support Force (PLASSF), created in the 2015 reorganisation of the military, is principally dedicated to information warfare, echoing the part of US space doctrine which states that 'access to space enables military operations in other domains, while denying space to the enemy undercuts its ability to conduct coherent military operations'.[25] Other states with significant military sectors are either partners or players in the development of space as 'a warfighting domain', as the USSF Capstone Publication on doctrine declares space to be: 'The Space Capstone Publication opens with the declaration that space is a warfighting domain. This assertion has tremendous repercussions for force structure, budget decisions, public and international perceptions, and, perhaps most significantly, for the culture of the newest military service'.[26]

The distinction between weapon systems deployed in space and 'space support functions' such as satellite-facilitated communications and surveillance, although real and therefore useful when invoked in legal discussions concerning whether a state has violated space law norms and aspirations, is a fudge, for in practice 'support functions' are as much weapons as 'kinetic' entities such as ASAT missiles, kamikaze satellites, or a military spacecraft such as the Boeing X-20 Dyna-Soar.[27] Using 'non-kinetic' technologies of jamming, hacking, laser-blinding, and triggering self-destruction of others' satellites has the same effect as shooting them down. In-space and Earth-to-space attack is joined by attack on Earth-based 'uplink and downlink' space facilities in making space a warfighting domain. In fact, given the importance of space-based assets such as surveillance and communications to terrestrial combat operations, the truth is that space is not a *separate* warfighting domain but a projection and continuation of Earth as the scene of almost continual warfare, somewhere or other, in most years of any decade.

These remarks do more than enough to illustrate the point that as resource extraction in space develops – by public and private entities, jointly or separately, though with an increment of risk introduced by the latter – the already-established fact of space as an arena of military activity raises to a high degree the possibility that conflict will arise from commercial competition and the establishment of permanent facilities in space and on celestial bodies. The terrestrial precedents are too clear for this not to be a serious fear. It is dramatised by the crucial point already made: that the 1967 Treaty is inadequate to the situation that has developed since its day. It does not prevent private agencies from claiming ownership of regions of space and the moon or other celestial bodies. It does not define where space begins, which complicates legal questions about militarisation. It bans nuclear weapons and 'weapons of mass destruction', but does not ban either conventional weapons nor the new-technology weapons developed since the end of the 1970s, which is the latest date at which binding Treaty obligations were attempted by the UN.

In large part as a function of being out of date, important terms in the Treaty require clearer definition or replacement by more adequate terminology. The Treaty did not establish an enforcement body, as UNCLOS has sought to do with the Seabed Authority. Debate over such matters as insurance and compensation for accidents or damage caused by space debris or other factors, injury to space crew or tourists, protection of privacy against the use of space-based surveillance and monitoring of terrestrial populations, the vulnerability of the internet and computer systems to space-based devices created to hack and jam – all this and more lie outside the effectiveness of the Treaty itself.

Work to address this problem is undertaken by the UN's Committee on the Peaceful Uses of Outer Space (COPUOS), an *ad hoc* body first set up by the General Assembly in December 1958. It is assisted and advised by the UN's Office for Outer Space Affairs (UNOOSA).[28] COPUOS has two subcommittees, one focused on space technology, the other on space law. The latter has the considerable achievements to its credit of the Agreements supplementary to the Treaty (on the rescue of astronauts, liability for damage caused by space objects, and registration of space objects). It is also the source of the ill-fated 1979 Agreement Governing the Activities of States on the Moon.

In COPUOS's 2022 meeting of its legal subcommittee the matter of resource exploitation in space – a perennial – iterated a number of points associated with the Treaty's crucial 'peaceful uses for the benefit of all mankind' commitment: among other things, that there should be an international regime to govern the exploitation of natural resources on the moon and other bodies, that information about the technological developments for doing so, and the activities undertaken, should be shared, that environmental concerns including the risks of contamination on Earth by materials returned to it from space should be properly taken into account, and – in light of the Artemis Accords and their implications – that 'unilateral regulation of space resource activities in national legislation or through the development of agreements outside the multilateral setting of the Committee could lead to fragmentation of international space law, which would inevitably lead to significant difficulties in or the impossibility of harmonizing such norms at the international level at subsequent stages of the development of activities for the exploration, exploitation and utilization of space resources'.[29]

This last point reinforces the problem with the existing framework, despite the good efforts of COPUOS to maintain the effectiveness of the principles of the Treaty and its associated instruments. Space technology, the profit motive, Earth geopolitics, and national prestige imperatives have whisked the situation beyond the current ability not just of the world's states individually but of the international structures set up to contain it. A space Wild West is coming into existence. The consequences for peace and stability on Earth, already tenuous on conventional grounds (think of Ukraine, China–US relations, recurrent local meltdowns in the Middle East, Sudan, and elsewhere), could be, and too likely will be, as petrol onto a fire.

The 1967 Treaty was in essence a Cold War arms control treaty. Its limitations and ambiguities led directly to such outcomes as the US Commercial Space Launch Competitiveness Act of 2015, and similar national legislation being contemplated or enacted in India, Japan, China, and Russia, which as COPUOS warns is a major step in fragmenting space law and increasing the potential for friction in space.

# CONCLUSION

## WHAT WILL HAPPEN? WHAT CAN BE DONE?

The Antarctic Treaty System has provided a significant measure of protection for the Antarctic because of the deliberate fudge of its Article IV. As mentioned in Chapter 3, none of the parties to the treaty exercised its right to call for a review in 1991, an abstention which has the effect of leaving the treaty in indefinite operation, although the ban on mining on the continent of Antarctica expires in 2048. The Antarctic Treaty states openly what all international agreements implicitly rest upon, namely, the understanding that they work only as long as it suits the parties to them to observe them. This is the 'expediency' time-bomb lodged in all of them – the danger of treaties being broken whenever it is expedient for one of the parties to do so. As the examples given in Chapters 3 and 4 show, the imperatives of economics and state sovereignty claims are a standing risk to detonation of that bomb.

When we consider the 1967 Outer Space Treaty we have to ask: what will be found when the establishment of bases, the commencement of commercial operations, mining, and more detailed on-site exploration, take place? How important will the moon and Mars become? What if resources are found that might trigger new versions of gold rushes, new urgencies of occupation and possession? What economic imperatives, what degrees of national pride, what possibilities of conflict and hostilities arising from competition and arms-race-type scrambles might occur?

These speculative questions are not so much the point as the wholly unspeculative observation – unspeculative because of the weight of empirical proof afforded by history – that it is more rather than less probable that if anything of economic significance is found in space, it will trigger competition, followed by the risk that competition will lead to conflict. This is the nub of everything we know of the human story, almost to the point of being a law of history. Add the thought that it is more rather than less probable that there *will* be things found in space that profit-seekers and governments on Earth will want to claim – the minerals and water ice already detected on the moon support the expectation – and we have the ingredients of the anticipated toxic brew.

Return your gaze to the Antarctic. There are three main types of reason why it has not so far been subjected to the 'law of history' just mentioned: (a) Such resources as are known to be there are hard to get because of the harsh environment and the difficulty of extracting or otherwise harvesting them. (b) The strength of opinion about the Antarctic – the unspoiled continent which is the common heritage of humankind, a view promoted by the eloquence and determination of a protective environmental lobby – has so far been maintained. (c) The unpalatable consequences of a revival of sovereignty claims, and the international discord that would attend efforts by any of the claimants to exert its claimed sovereign right to engage in commercial exploitation of resources, are powerful disincentives to either.

Similar considerations will hold the line on the *principles* of the 1967 Treaty for a time. But unlike the Antarctic Treaty, for the 1967 Treaty the (a) consideration plays no part in light of technological advances, it does not have a (b) consideration in its support, and (c) is anyway regarded as inapplicable to space. Given that the expediency bomb is lodged even in the Antarctic Treaty, and that it is not hard to imagine a time when the (a)–(c) considerations will not withstand some extreme need to exploit the Antarctic's resources, the same applies with even greater force to the Outer Space Treaty.

The Antarctic Treaty and the UN's treaties on space and the sea were products of an important moment in history: the decades following the two world wars 1914–18 and 1939–45, the failure of the League of Nations to prevent the second, and the horrific atrocities committed during the course of the latter. Together these prompted creation of the United Nations organisation, which in the years and decades following its official birth on 24 October 1945 tried to build a framework for peace and justice (neither possible without the other) that would rescue the world from its tragic propensity for conflict. It adopted not just the Declaration of Human Rights and its subsequent set of associated conventions – together constituting an International Bill of Human Rights with the force of international law – but, over the next decades, a set of measures designed to protect and further the interests of humankind and its planetary home more generally – hence the treaties discussed in this book.

Although high ethical principle was one significant motivation for these measures, it has to be acknowledged that the chief driver for them was Cold War tension, and the application of rational self-interest by the major powers, principally the US and the USSR, to control the potential for conflict by mutually imposing and accepting limits on some of the activities that could cause it. If there had not been a nuclear threat and an extremely fragile international equilibrium (vented by tragic proxy wars as in Vietnam), would these treaties have been signed? It is difficult to achieve international agreement requiring any form of sacrifice – and not just financial sacrifice: the sacrifice of power, influence, territory, security, 'face', are hard for any states to accept, and they usually do so only when comprehensively defeated in war – so that without the pressure of so serious risk as devastating nuclear conflict, securing the treaties might have taken longer, if it happened at all.

That these treaties were signed is therefore a silver lining of the Cold War. One of the notable features of them is their constantly iterated focus on peace. By this of course was meant *military* peace, the absence of *hot* war, of actual violent conflict. Proponents and drafters of the treaties doubtless believed that observance of them would be a confidence-building measure; for example, if Soviet astronauts rescued endangered US astronauts out beyond the Kármán Line, or vice versa, it would help to reduce tensions and foster more fraternal relations. The 1967 Treaty encourages cooperation and open access to scientific exploration of space and celestial bodies, as the Antarctic Treaty does with regard to Antarctica. This is obviously good. And it prohibits siting military bases on the moon and Mars, or testing weapon systems there. This is also obviously good – but this time it is, as with the Antarctic Treaty, in fact a statement of aspiration, not a guarantee that international tensions will not prompt withdrawal of one or more parties from the treaty, or violation of its terms. It is not such a guarantee because it cannot be. The international realm is an anarchy, where restraint is enforced only by national self-interest, and when the latter is not best served by adhering to agreements, the agreements will be worth little or nothing.[1]

This is where the imminent prospect of commercial competition in space becomes a concern. In explicitly treating space and celestial bodies as non-rivalrous and non-excludable goods, the Space Treaty at the same time permits unconstrained commercial activity, and therefore the potential for sharp competition between agencies, public or private, targeting the same resources. The Treaty tries to make the governments of the private agencies' home nations responsible for them, a more rather than less vain hope in an age of mighty international corporations which, on Earth, are practically a law unto themselves. The absence of any provision for *commercial* peace in the form of regulation of commercial activity in space therefore leaves open repeats of those aspects of capitalism that in their unbridled form have prompted adoption of regulatory regimes on Earth because of the painful lessons learned when capitalism is nothing more than the licensing of greed and a graceless rush for money-profit above all other considerations.[2]

In light of these facts, treating space as a *terra nullius* with no regulation of commercial exploitation is a sure recipe for problems both in space and on Earth, for – to repeat, as one endlessly must – we have ample evidence of what uncontrolled scrambles for advantage and profit typically do. For prudential reasons, if for no other, ensuring that space does not become a reason for disturbance of peace in the *military* sense requires ensuring that *commercial* peace is preserved there too. That would seem to be plain common sense.

But there are further considerations, which prompt some novel thoughts about what humanity should add to its conceptual resources as it reaches out into space. A way to put the point is to look at what must assuredly be the right answer to the question that is this book's title, 'Who owns the moon?' As the foregoing discussions show, the answer is unequivocally 'No one'. What is needed for this answer *not* to be a source of the problems just identified – that is, not to be the trigger for an anarchic competitive scramble for advantage and profit – is a recognition that although no one *owns* the moon, nevertheless because it is part of the 'common inheritance of mankind' we are all *responsible* for it. The idea that one can be responsible for something over which one has no rights or claims is in fact already implicit in the idea of humankind's relationship with (for example) wild elephants and gorillas: we do not own them, have no rights to them, but we are responsible for their welfare and survival.

This emphasises an ethical and legal dimension to agents[3] which looks asymmetrical: you do not own and cannot make claims on X but you are responsible for the welfare of X, or for the consequences of any actions taken with respect to X. The idea of a '*common interest* of mankind' thus implies a *common responsibility* of mankind. Something cannot plausibly be an interest – that is, something one cares about, regards as having some kind of value or significance, recognises its existence as advantageous or worthwhile in an identifiable respect – while its welfare, even its very existence, is at the same time a matter of indifference, requiring nothing of one in the way of an exercise of that interest. (Examples of 'exercising an interest' would be campaigning to protect the gorillas' habitat, raising funds to combat ivory poaching, lobbying for regulation of commercial activity in space.)

And in this sense, despite the nature of the noted asymmetry between ownership and responsibility, humankind can nevertheless be said to have a *collective right to the common good in question being appropriately considered* at all times and, when necessary, actively protected – a point that can alternatively be put by saying that mankind collectively has a *right to the protection of its interest* in that common good.

This accordingly raises another important and even more novel point, relating to the UN declarations and treaties making 'humankind' a legal subject, a *person* with rights and responsibilities, fully possessed of *locus standi* (the right to be a party to e.g. relevant court proceedings) and thus an entity entitled to representation both at law and in general. This entails that humankind *as such* should have lawyers or at least representatives, appointed to act on behalf of its common interests, its common heritage, and the global good. In the ideal it might be said that the UN does or should play this role, but despite the great good that comes from the UN in the way of the aspirations it tirelessly defends, it is all but powerless against the recalcitrance of individual states.

The UN declarations and treaties already define, both explicitly and by implication, what would be actionable in the way of humankind's collective interests, because their application already – though only in part – explicitly shadows such a proceeding by the various means it has for dealing with breaches of treaties: imposing sanctions, passing formal Security Council censures, carrying out peace-keeping operations with member-state militaries, while member states themselves can seek adjudications in appropriate courts and tribunals if affected by another member state's failure to observe a treaty obligation. The UN provision that deals with treaty breaches is the Vienna Convention on the Law of Treaties (1969). Its Article 26, entitled *pacta sunt servanda*, 'agreements must be kept', states 'Every treaty in force is binding upon the parties to it and must be performed by them in good faith.'[4] But this Convention, the Antarctic Treaty, UNCLOS, and the 1967 Outer Space Treaty all have a mighty opponent: the self-interest of states and private actors such as corporations. The vulnerability of agreements and aspirations to self-interest is even greater in outer space than in Antarctica or on and underneath the high seas: unless there is something available to humankind that is more powerful than partisan self-interest – in its related guises of the profit motive, ambitions for power, personal or national prestige, and the forces of history that create resentments and alliances – the 'tragedy' in the 'tragedy of the commons' in space could, and probably will, be great.

The task that faces the world is finding the 'something' that will avoid such an outcome – that will make treaties and agreements effective, and space and Earth itself thereby secure. Whatever it is, it will involve seeing that the self-interest of humanity as a whole requires that *partisan* self-interest – the self-interest of sections of humanity in opposition to other sections of humanity – has to end. This will take maturity and wisdom, neither of which has evolved to a sufficient degree so far, though the aspirations of UN treaties in their admirably persistent way encourage both. Theodor Adorno memorably said that humankind has 'grown cleverer but not wiser' over time, as demonstrated by its development of the spear into the guided missile, using increased technological cleverness to continue the lunacy of war; his remark identifies the key respect in which humanity's self-management has to improve – to put it bluntly, by growing up. It is an existential matter. There is an example of how it might be done in the comity of nations that is the European Union. All history weighs against the prospects of the EU's achievement in that regard becoming worldwide. And if history wins, the result will be the tragedy of the commons not just in space, but at home on Earth.

# APPENDIX 1

## THE UN OUTER SPACE TREATY 1967

### Treaty on Principles Governing the Activities of States in the Exploration and Use of Outer Space, including the Moon and Other Celestial Bodies

*The States Parties to this Treaty,*

*Inspired* by the great prospects opening up before mankind as a result of man's entry into outer space,

*Recognizing* the common interest of all mankind in the progress of the exploration and use of outer space for peaceful purposes,

*Believing* that the exploration and use of outer space should be carried on for the benefit of all peoples irrespective of the degree of their economic or scientific development,

*Desiring* to contribute to broad international cooperation in the scientific as well as the legal aspects of the exploration and use of outer space for peaceful purposes,

*Believing* that such cooperation will contribute to the development of mutual understanding and to the strengthening of friendly relations between States and peoples,

*Recalling* resolution 1962 (XVIII), entitled 'Declaration of Legal Principles Governing the Activities of States in the Exploration and Use of Outer Space', which was adopted unanimously by the United Nations General Assembly on 13 December 1963,

*Recalling* resolution 1884 (XVIII), calling upon States to refrain from placing in orbit around the Earth any objects carrying nuclear weapons or any other kinds of weapons of mass destruction or from installing such weapons on celestial bodies, which was adopted unanimously by the United Nations General Assembly on 17 October 1963,

*Taking* account of United Nations General Assembly resolution 110 (II) of 3 November 1947, which condemned propaganda designed or likely to provoke or encourage any threat to the peace, breach of the peace or act of aggression, and considering that the aforementioned resolution is applicable to outer space,

*Convinced* that a Treaty on Principles Governing the Activities of States in the Exploration and Use of Outer Space, including the Moon and Other Celestial Bodies, will further the purposes and principles of the Charter of the United Nations,

*Have agreed on the following:*

## Article I

The exploration and use of outer space, including the Moon and other celestial bodies, shall be carried out for the benefit and in the interests of all countries, irrespective of their degree of economic or scientific development, and shall be the province of all mankind.

Outer space, including the Moon and other celestial bodies, shall be free for exploration and use by all States without discrimination of any kind, on a basis of equality and in accordance with international law, and there shall be free access to all areas of celestial bodies.

There shall be freedom of scientific investigation in outer space, including the Moon and other celestial bodies, and States shall facilitate and encourage international cooperation in such investigation.

## Article II

Outer space, including the Moon and other celestial bodies, is not subject to national appropriation by claim of sovereignty, by means of use or occupation, or by any other means.

## Article III

States Parties to the Treaty shall carry on activities in the exploration and use of outer space, including the Moon and other celestial bodies, in accordance with international law, including the Charter of the United Nations, in the interest of maintaining international peace and security and promoting international cooperation and understanding.

### Article IV

States Parties to the Treaty undertake not to place in orbit around the Earth any objects carrying nuclear weapons or any other kinds of weapons of mass destruction, install such weapons on celestial bodies, or station such weapons in outer space in any other manner.

The Moon and other celestial bodies shall be used by all States Parties to the Treaty exclusively for peaceful purposes. The establishment of military bases, installations and fortifications, the testing of any type of weapons and the conduct of military manoeuvres on celestial bodies shall be forbidden. The use of military personnel for scientific research or for any other peaceful purposes shall not be prohibited. The use of any equipment or facility necessary for peaceful exploration of the Moon and other celestial bodies shall also not be prohibited.

### Article V

States Parties to the Treaty shall regard astronauts as envoys of mankind in outer space and shall render to them all possible assistance in the event of accident, distress, or emergency landing on the territory of another State Party or on the high seas. When astronauts make such a landing, they shall be safely and promptly returned to the State of registry of their space vehicle.

In carrying on activities in outer space and on celestial bodies, the astronauts of one State Party shall render all possible assistance to the astronauts of other States Parties.

States Parties to the Treaty shall immediately inform the other States Parties to the Treaty or the Secretary-General of the United Nations of any phenomena they discover in outer space, including the Moon and other celestial bodies, which could constitute a danger to the life or health of astronauts.

## Article VI

States Parties to the Treaty shall bear international responsibility for national activities in outer space, including the Moon and other celestial bodies, whether such activities are carried on by governmental agencies or by non-governmental entities, and for assuring that national activities are carried out in conformity with the provisions set forth in the present Treaty. The activities of non-governmental entities in outer space, including the Moon and other celestial bodies, shall require authorization and continuing supervision by the appropriate State Party to the Treaty. When activities are carried on in outer space, including the Moon and other celestial bodies, by an international organization, responsibility for compliance with this Treaty shall be borne both by the international organization and by the States Parties to the Treaty participating in such organization.

## Article VII

Each State Party to the Treaty that launches or procures the launching of an object into outer space, including the Moon and other celestial bodies, and each State Party from whose territory or facility an object is launched, is internationally liable for damage to another State Party to the Treaty or to its natural or juridical persons by such object or its component parts on the Earth, in air space or in outer space, including the Moon and other celestial bodies.

Article VIII

A State Party to the Treaty on whose registry an object launched into outer space is carried shall retain jurisdiction and control over such object, and over any personnel thereof, while in outer space or on a celestial body. Ownership of objects launched into outer space, including objects landed or constructed on a celestial body, and of their component parts, is not affected by their presence in outer space or on a celestial body or by their return to the Earth. Such objects or component parts found beyond the limits of the State Party to the Treaty on whose registry they are carried shall be returned to that State Party, which shall, upon request, furnish identifying data prior to their return.

Article IX

In the exploration and use of outer space, including the Moon and other celestial bodies, States Parties to the Treaty shall be guided by the principle of cooperation and mutual assistance and shall conduct all their activities in outer space, including the Moon and other celestial bodies, with due regard to the corresponding interests of all other States Parties to the Treaty. States Parties to the Treaty shall pursue studies of outer space, including the Moon and other celestial bodies, and conduct exploration of them so as to avoid their harmful contamination and also adverse changes in the environment of the Earth resulting from the introduction of extraterrestrial matter and, where necessary, shall adopt appropriate measures for this purpose. If a State Party to the Treaty has reason to believe that an activity or experiment planned by it or its nationals in outer space, including the Moon and other celestial bodies, would cause potentially harmful interference with activities of other States Parties in the peaceful exploration and use of outer space, including the Moon and other celestial bodies, it shall undertake appropriate international consultations before proceeding with any such activity or experiment. A State Party to the Treaty which has reason to believe that an activity or experiment planned by another State Party in outer space, including the Moon and other celestial bodies, would cause potentially harmful interference with activities in the peaceful exploration and use of outer space, including the Moon and other celestial bodies, may request consultation concerning the activity or experiment.

## Article X

In order to promote international cooperation in the exploration and use of outer space, including the Moon and other celestial bodies, in conformity with the purposes of this Treaty, the States Parties to the Treaty shall consider on a basis of equality any requests by other States Parties to the Treaty to be afforded an opportunity to observe the flight of space objects launched by those States.

The nature of such an opportunity for observation and the conditions under which it could be afforded shall be determined by agreement between the States concerned.

## Article XI

In order to promote international cooperation in the peaceful exploration and use of outer space, States Parties to the Treaty conducting activities in outer space, including the Moon and other celestial bodies, agree to inform the Secretary-General of the United Nations as well as the public and the international scientific community, to the greatest extent feasible and practicable, of the nature, conduct, locations and results of such activities. On receiving the said information, the Secretary-General of the United Nations should be prepared to disseminate it immediately and effectively.

## Article XII

All stations, installations, equipment and space vehicles on the Moon and other celestial bodies shall be open to representatives of other States Parties to the Treaty on a basis of reciprocity. Such representatives shall give reasonable advance notice of a projected visit, in order that appropriate consultations may be held and that maximum precautions may be taken to assure safety and to avoid interference with normal operations in the facility to be visited.

## Article XIII

The provisions of this Treaty shall apply to the activities of States Parties to the Treaty in the exploration and use of outer space, including the Moon and other celestial bodies, whether such activities are carried on by a single State Party to the Treaty or jointly with other States, including cases where they are carried on within the framework of international intergovernmental organizations.

Any practical questions arising in connection with activities carried on by international intergovernmental organizations in the exploration and use of outer space, including the Moon and other celestial bodies, shall be resolved by the States Parties to the Treaty either with the appropriate international organization or with one or more States members of that international organization, which are Parties to this Treaty.

### Article XIV

1. This Treaty shall be open to all States for signature. Any State which does not sign this Treaty before its entry into force in accordance with paragraph 3 of this article may accede to it at any time.

2. This Treaty shall be subject to ratification by signatory States. Instruments of ratification and instruments of accession shall be deposited with the Governments of the Union of Soviet Socialist Republics, the United Kingdom of Great Britain and Northern Ireland and the United States of America, which are hereby designated the Depositary Governments.

3. This Treaty shall enter into force upon the deposit of instruments of ratification by five Governments including the

Governments designated as Depositary Governments under this Treaty.

4. For States whose instruments of ratification or accession are deposited subsequent to the entry into force of this Treaty, it shall enter into force on the date of the deposit of their instruments of ratification or accession.

5. The Depositary Governments shall promptly inform all signatory and acceding States of the date of each signature, the date of deposit of each instrument of ratification of and accession to this Treaty, the date of its entry into force and other notices.

6. This Treaty shall be registered by the Depositary Governments pursuant to Article 102 of the Charter of the United Nations.

## Article XV

Any State Party to the Treaty may propose amendments to this Treaty. Amendments shall enter into force for each State Party to the Treaty accepting the amendments upon their acceptance by a majority of the States Parties to the Treaty and thereafter for each remaining State Party to the Treaty on the date of acceptance by it.

## Article XVI

Any State Party to the Treaty may give notice of its withdrawal from the Treaty one year after its entry into force by written notification to the Depositary Governments. Such withdrawal shall take effect one year from the date of receipt of this notification.

### Article XVII

This Treaty, of which the Chinese, English, French, Russian and Spanish texts are equally authentic, shall be deposited in the archives of the Depositary Governments. Duly certified copies of this Treaty shall be transmitted by the Depositary Governments to the Governments of the signatory and acceding States.

IN WITNESS WHEREOF the undersigned, duly authorized, have signed this Treaty.

DONE in triplicate, at the cities of London, Moscow and Washington, D.C., the twenty-seventh day of January, one thousand nine hundred and sixty-seven.

# APPENDIX 2

## THE ANTARCTIC TREATY 1961

The Governments of Argentina, Australia, Belgium, Chile, the French Republic, Japan, New Zealand, Norway, the Union of South Africa, the Union of Soviet Socialist Republics, the United Kingdom of Great Britain and Northern Ireland, and the United States of America,

Recognizing that it is in the interest of all mankind that Antarctica shall continue for ever to be used exclusively for peaceful purposes and shall not become the scene or object of international discord;

Acknowledging the substantial contributions to scientific knowledge resulting from international cooperation in scientific investigation in Antarctica;

Convinced that the establishment of a firm foundation for the continuation and development of such cooperation on the basis of freedom of scientific investigation in Antarctica as applied during the International Geophysical Year accords with the interests of science and the progress of all mankind;

Convinced also that a treaty ensuring the use of Antarctica for peaceful purposes only and the continuance of international harmony in Antarctica will further the purposes and principles embodied in the Charter of the United Nations;

Have agreed as follows:

### Article I

1. Antarctica shall be used for peaceful purposes only. There shall be prohibited, inter alia, any measures of a military nature, such as the establishment of military bases and fortifications, the carrying out of military maneuvers, as well as the testing of any type of weapons.

2. The present Treaty shall not prevent the use of military personnel or equipment for scientific research or for any other peaceful purpose.

### Article II

Freedom of scientific investigation in Antarctica and cooperation toward that end, as applied during the International Geophysical Year, shall continue, subject to the provisions of the present Treaty.

### Article III

1. In order to promote international cooperation in scientific investigation in Antarctica, as provided for in Article II of the

present Treaty, the Contracting Parties agree that, to the greatest extent feasible and practicable:

(a) information regarding plans for scientific programs in Antarctica shall be exchanged to permit maximum economy and efficiency of operations;
(b) scientific personnel shall be exchanged in Antarctica between expeditions and stations;
(c) scientific observations and results from Antarctica shall be exchanged and made freely available.

2. In implementing this Article, every encouragement shall be given to the establishment of cooperative working relations with those Specialized Agencies of the United Nations and other international organizations having a scientific or technical interest in Antarctica.

## Article IV

1. Nothing contained in the present Treaty shall be interpreted as:

(a) a renunciation by any Contracting Party of previously asserted rights of or claims to territorial sovereignty in Antarctica;
(b) a renunciation or diminution by any Contracting Party of any basis of claim to territorial sovereignty in Antarctica which it may have whether as a result of its activities or those of its nationals in Antarctica, or otherwise;
(c) prejudicing the position of any Contracting Party as regards its recognition or non-recognition of any other State's right

of or claim or basis of claim to territorial sovereignty in Antarctica.

2. No acts or activities taking place while the present Treaty is in force shall constitute a basis for asserting, supporting or denying a claim to territorial sovereignty in Antarctica or create any rights of sovereignty in Antarctica. No new claim, or enlargement of an existing claim, to territorial sovereignty in Antarctica shall be asserted while the present Treaty is in force.

Article V

1. Any nuclear explosions in Antarctica and the disposal there of radioactive waste material shall be prohibited.

2. In the event of the conclusion of international agreements concerning the use of nuclear energy, including nuclear explosions and the disposal of radioactive waste material, to which all of the Contracting Parties whose representatives are entitled to participate in the meetings provided for under Article IX are parties, the rules established under such agreements shall apply in Antarctica.

Article VI

The provisions of the present Treaty shall apply to the area south of 60° South Latitude, including all ice shelves, but nothing in the present Treaty shall prejudice or in any way affect the rights, or the exercise of the rights, of any State under international law with regard to the high seas within that area.

## Article VII

1. In order to promote the objectives and ensure the observance of the provisions of the present Treaty, each Contracting Party whose representatives are entitled to participate in the meetings referred to in Article IX of the Treaty shall have the right to designate observers to carry out any inspection provided for by the present Article. Observers shall be nationals of the Contracting Parties which designate them. The names of observers shall be communicated to every other Contracting Party having the right to designate observers, and like notice shall be given of the termination of their appointment.

2. Each observer designated in accordance with the provisions of paragraph 1 of this Article shall have complete freedom of access at any time to any or all areas of Antarctica.

3. All areas of Antarctica, including all stations, installations and equipment within those areas, and all ships and aircraft at points of discharging or embarking cargoes or personnel in Antarctica, shall be open at all times to inspection by any observers designated in accordance with paragraph 1 of this Article.

4. Aerial observation may be carried out at any time over any or all areas of Antarctica by any of the Contracting Parties having the right to designate observers.

5. Each Contracting Party shall, at the time when the present Treaty enters into force for it, inform the other Contracting Parties, and thereafter shall give them notice in advance, of

(a) all expeditions to and within Antarctica, on the part of its ships or nationals, and all expeditions to Antarctica organized in or proceeding from its territory;
(b) all stations in Antarctica occupied by its nationals; and
(c) any military personnel or equipment intended to be introduced by it into Antarctica subject to the conditions prescribed in paragraph 2 of Article I of the present Treaty.

## Article VIII

1. In order to facilitate the exercise of their functions under the present Treaty, and without prejudice to the respective positions of the Contracting Parties relating to jurisdiction over all other persons in Antarctica, observers designated under paragraph 1 of Article VII and scientific personnel exchanged under subparagraph 1(b) of Article III of the Treaty, and members of the staffs accompanying any such persons, shall be subject only to the jurisdiction of the Contracting Party of which they are nationals in respect of all acts or omissions occurring while they are in Antarctica for the purpose of exercising their functions.

2. Without prejudice to the provisions of paragraph 1 of this Article, and pending the adoption of measures in pursuance of subparagraph 1(e) of Article IX, the Contracting Parties concerned in any case of dispute with regard to the exercise of jurisdiction in Antarctica shall immediately consult together with a view to reaching a mutually acceptable solution.

## Article IX

1. Representatives of the Contracting Parties named in the preamble to the present Treaty shall meet at the City of Canberra within two months after the date of entry into force of the Treaty, and thereafter at suitable intervals and places, for the purpose of exchanging information, consulting together on matters of common interest pertaining to Antarctica, and formulating and considering, and recommending to their Governments, measures in furtherance of the principles and objectives of the Treaty, including measures regarding:

(a) use of Antarctica for peaceful purposes only;
(b) facilitation of scientific research in Antarctica;
(c) facilitation of international scientific cooperation in Antarctica;
(d) facilitation of the exercise of the rights of inspection provided for in Article VII of the Treaty;
(e) questions relating to the exercise of jurisdiction in Antarctica;
(f) preservation and conservation of living resources in Antarctica.

2. Each Contracting Party which has become a party to the present Treaty by accession under Article XIII shall be entitled to appoint representatives to participate in the meetings referred to in paragraph 1 of the present Article, during such time as that Contracting Party demonstrates its interest in Antarctica by conducting substantial scientific research activity there, such as the establishment of a

scientific station or the despatch of a scientific expedition.

3. Reports from the observers referred to in Article VII of the present Treaty shall be transmitted to the representatives of the Contracting Parties participating in the meetings referred to in paragraph 1 of the present Article.

4. The measures referred to in paragraph 1 of this Article shall become effective when approved by all the Contracting Parties whose representatives were entitled to participate in the meetings held to consider those measures.

5. Any or all of the rights established in the present Treaty may be exercised as from the date of entry into force of the Treaty whether or not any measures facilitating the exercise of such rights have been proposed, considered or approved as provided in this Article.

Article X

Each of the Contracting Parties undertakes to exert appropriate efforts, consistent with the Charter of the United Nations, to the end that no one engages in any activity in Antarctica contrary to the principles or purposes of the present Treaty.

Article XI

1. If any dispute arises between two or more of the Contracting Parties concerning the interpretation or application of the present Treaty, those Contracting Parties shall consult among

themselves with a view to having the dispute resolved by negotiation, inquiry, mediation, conciliation, arbitration, judicial settlement or other peaceful means of their own choice.

2. Any dispute of this character not so resolved shall, with the consent, in each case, of all parties to the dispute, be referred to the International Court of Justice for settlement; but failure to reach agreement on reference to the International Court shall not absolve parties to the dispute from the responsibility of continuing to seek to resolve it by any of the various peaceful means referred to in paragraph 1 of this Article.

## Article XII

1. (a) The present Treaty may be modified or amended at any time by unanimous agreement of the Contracting Parties whose representatives are entitled to participate in the meetings provided for under Article IX. Any such modification or amendment shall enter into force when the depositary Government has received notice from all such Contracting Parties that they have ratified it.

(b) Such modification or amendment shall thereafter enter into force as to any other Contracting Party when notice of ratification by it has been received by the depositary Government. Any such Contracting Party from which no notice of ratification is received within a period of two years from the date of entry into force of the modification or amendment in accordance with the provisions of subparagraph 1(a) of this Article shall be deemed to have withdrawn from the present Treaty on the date of the expiration of such period.

2. (a) If after the expiration of thirty years from the date of entry into force of the present Treaty, any of the Contracting Parties whose representatives are entitled to participate in the meetings provided for under Article IX so requests by a communication addressed to the depositary Government, a Conference of all the Contracting Parties shall be held as soon as practicable to review the operation of the Treaty.

(b) Any modification or amendment to the present Treaty which is approved at such a Conference by a majority of the Contracting Parties there represented, including a majority of those whose representatives are entitled to participate in the meetings provided for under Article IX, shall be communicated by the depositary Government to all the Contracting Parties immediately after the termination of the Conference and shall enter into force in accordance with the provisions of paragraph 1 of the present Article.

(c) If any such modification or amendment has not entered into force in accordance with the provisions of subparagraph 1(a) of this Article within a period of two years after the date of its communication to all the Contracting Parties, any Contracting Party may at any time after the expiration of that period give notice to the depositary Government of its withdrawal from the present Treaty; and such withdrawal shall take effect two years after the receipt of the notice by the depositary Government.

## Article XIII

1. The present Treaty shall be subject to ratification by the signatory States. It shall be open for accession by any State which is a Member of the United Nations, or by any other State which may be invited to accede to the Treaty with the consent of all the Contracting Parties whose representatives are entitled to participate in the meetings provided for under Article IX of the Treaty.

2. Ratification of or accession to the present Treaty shall be effected by each State in accordance with its constitutional processes.

3. Instruments of ratification and instruments of accession shall be deposited with the Government of the United States of America, hereby designated as the depositary Government.

4. The depositary Government shall inform all signatory and acceding States of the date of each deposit of an instrument of ratification or accession, and the date of entry into force of the Treaty and of any modification or amendment thereto.

5. Upon the deposit of instruments of ratification by all the signatory States, the present Treaty shall enter into force for those States and for States which have deposited instruments of accession. Thereafter the Treaty shall enter into force for any acceding State upon the deposit of its instrument of accession.

6. The present Treaty shall be registered by the depositary Government pursuant to Article 102 of the Charter of the United Nations.

Article XIV

The present Treaty, done in the English, French, Russian and Spanish languages, each version being equally authentic, shall be deposited in the archives of the Government of the United States of America, which shall transmit duly certified copies thereof to the Governments of the signatory and acceding States.

# APPENDIX 3

## THE UN CONVENTION ON THE LAW OF THE SEA 1982, EXCERPTS

The following excerpts from the lengthy and exhaustive UNCLOS are selected for their interest in comparison to provisions, or their absence, in the 1961 Antarctic Treaty and the 1967 Outer Space Treaty. Reflection on the careful and detailed provisions of UNCLOS provide an indication of how a legal regime for outer space might better be formulated. In common with all other major UN treaties and conventions, however, UNCLOS is vulnerable to the non-compliance of parties whether signatories or not. In respect of its careful and exhaustive character, it is a model of what a rational and considered global agreement should be.

## PREAMBLE

The States Parties to this Convention,

Prompted by the desire to settle, in a spirit of mutual understanding and cooperation, all issues relating to the law of the sea and aware of the historic significance of this Convention as an important contribution to the maintenance of peace, justice and progress for all peoples of the world,

Noting that developments since the United Nations Conferences on the Law of the Sea held at Geneva in 1958 and 1960 have accentuated the need for a new and generally acceptable Convention on the law of the sea,

Conscious that the problems of ocean space are closely interrelated and need to be considered as a whole,

Recognizing the desirability of establishing through this Convention, with due regard for the sovereignty of all States, a legal order for the seas and oceans which will facilitate international communication, and will promote the peaceful uses of the seas and oceans, the equitable and efficient utilization of their resources, the conservation of their living resources, and the study, protection and preservation of the marine environment,

Bearing in mind that the achievement of these goals will contribute to the realization of a just and equitable international economic order which takes into account the interests and needs of mankind as a whole and, in particular, the special interests and needs of developing countries, whether coastal or land-locked,

Desiring by this Convention to develop the principles embodied in resolution 2749 (XXV) of 17 December 1970 in which the General Assembly of the United Nations solemnly declared inter alia that the area of the seabed and ocean floor and the subsoil thereof, beyond the limits of national jurisdiction, as well as its resources, are the common heritage of mankind, the exploration and exploitation of which shall be carried out for the benefit of mankind as a whole, irrespective of the geographical location of States,

Believing that the codification and progressive development of the law of the sea achieved in this Convention will contribute to the strengthening of peace, security, cooperation and friendly relations among all nations in conformity with the principles of justice and equal rights and will promote the economic and social advancement of all peoples of the world, in accordance with the Purposes and Principles of the United Nations as set forth in the Charter,

Affirming that matters not regulated by this Convention continue to be governed by the rules and principles of general international law,

Have agreed as follows . . .

Article 17 (and others for straits, archipelagic waters, etc.)
Right of innocent passage
Subject to this Convention, ships of all States, whether coastal or land-locked, enjoy the right of innocent passage . . .

Article 69
Right of land-locked States
1. Land-locked States shall have the right to participate, on an equitable basis, in the exploitation of an appropriate part of the surplus of the living resources of the exclusive economic zones of coastal States of the same subregion or region, taking into account the relevant economic and geographical circumstances of all the States concerned . . .

Article 70
Right of geographically disadvantaged States
1. Geographically disadvantaged States shall have the right to participate, on an equitable basis, in the exploitation of an appropriate part of the surplus of the living resources of the exclusive economic zones of coastal States of the same subregion or region, taking into account the relevant economic and geographical circumstances of all the States concerned . . .

Article 87

Freedom of the high seas
1. The high seas are open to all States, whether coastal or land-locked. Freedom of the high seas is exercised under the conditions laid down by this Convention and by other rules of

international law. It comprises, inter alia, both for coastal and land-locked States:

(a) freedom of navigation;
(b) freedom of over flight;
(c) freedom to lay submarine cables and pipelines, subject to Part VI;
(d) freedom to construct artificial islands and other installations permitted under international law, subject to Part VI;
(e) freedom of fishing, subject to the conditions laid down in section 2;
(f) freedom of scientific research, subject to Parts VI and XIII.

2. These freedoms shall be exercised by all States with due regard for the interests of other States in their exercise of the freedom of the high seas, and also with due regard for the rights under this Convention with respect to activities in the Area.

Article 88
Reservation of the high seas for peaceful purposes
The high seas shall be reserved for peaceful purposes.

Article 89
Invalidity of claims of sovereignty over the high seas
No State may validly purport to subject any part of the high seas to its sovereignty.

Article 90

Right of navigation

Every State, whether coastal or land-locked, has the right to sail ships flying its flag on the high seas.

Article 99

Prohibition of the transport of slaves

Every State shall take effective measures to prevent and punish the transport of slaves in ships authorized to fly its flag and to prevent the unlawful use of its flag for that purpose. Any slave taking refuge on board any ship, whatever its flag, shall ipso facto be free.

Article 116

Right to fish on the high seas

All States have the right for their nationals to engage in fishing on the high seas subject to:

(a) their treaty obligations;
(b) the rights and duties as well as the interests of coastal States provided for, inter alia, in article 63, paragraph 2, and articles 64 to 67; and
(c) the provisions of this section.

## Article 117
## Duty of States to adopt with respect to their nationals measures for the conservation of the living resources of the high seas

All States have the duty to take, or to cooperate with other States in taking, such measures for their respective nationals as may be necessary for the conservation of the living resources of the high seas.

## Article 118
## Cooperation of States in the conservation and management of living resources

States shall cooperate with each other in the conservation and management of living resources in the areas of the high seas. States whose nationals exploit identical living resources, or different living resources in the same area, shall enter into negotiations with a view to taking the measures necessary for the conservation of the living resources concerned.

## Article 136
## Common heritage of mankind

The Area and its resources are the common heritage of mankind.

## Article 137
## Legal status of the Area and its resources

1. No State shall claim or exercise sovereignty or sovereign rights over any part of the Area or its resources, nor shall any State or natural or juridical person appropriate any part

thereof. No such claim or exercise of sovereignty or sovereign rights nor such appropriation shall be recognized.

2. All rights in the resources of the Area are vested in mankind as a whole, on whose behalf the Authority shall act. These resources are not subject to alienation. The minerals recovered from the Area, however, may only be alienated in accordance with this Part and the rules, regulations and procedures of the Authority.

3. No State or natural or juridical person shall claim, acquire or exercise rights with respect to the minerals recovered from the Area except in accordance with this Part. Otherwise, no such claim, acquisition or exercise of such rights shall be recognized.

Article 138

General conduct of States in relation to the Area

The general conduct of States in relation to the Area shall be in accordance with the provisions of this Part, the principles embodied in the Charter of the United Nations and other rules of international law in the interests of maintaining peace and security and promoting international cooperation and mutual understanding.

Article 139

Responsibility to ensure compliance and liability for damage

1. States Parties shall have the responsibility to ensure that activities in the Area, whether carried out by States Parties,

or state enterprises or natural or juridical persons which possess the nationality of States Parties or are effectively controlled by them or their nationals, shall be carried out in conformity with this Part. The same responsibility applies to international organizations for activities in the Area carried out by such organizations.

2. Without prejudice to the rules of international law and Annex III, article 22, damage caused by the failure of a State Party or international organization to carry out its responsibilities under this Part shall entail liability; States Parties or international organizations acting together shall bear joint and several liability. A State Party shall not however be liable for damage caused by any failure to comply with this Part by a person whom it has sponsored under article 153, paragraph 2(b), if the State Party has taken all necessary and appropriate measures to secure effective compliance under article 153, paragraph 4, and Annex III, article 4, paragraph 4.

3. States Parties that are members of international organizations shall take appropriate measures to ensure the implementation of this article with respect to such organizations.

### Article 140
### Benefit of mankind

1. Activities in the Area shall, as specifically provided for in this Part, be carried out for the benefit of mankind as a whole, irrespective of the geographical location of States, whether coastal or land-locked, and taking into particular consideration the interests and needs of developing States and of

peoples who have not attained full independence or other self-governing status recognized by the United Nations in accordance with General Assembly resolution 1514 (XV) and other relevant General Assembly resolutions.

2. The Authority shall provide for the equitable sharing of financial and other economic benefits derived from activities in the Area through any appropriate mechanism, on a non-discriminatory basis, in accordance with article 160, paragraph 2(f)(i).

Article 141
Use of the Area exclusively for peaceful purposes
The Area shall be open to use exclusively for peaceful purposes by all States, whether coastal or land-locked, without discrimination and without prejudice to the other provisions of this Part.

Article 142
Rights and legitimate interests of coastal States
1. Activities in the Area, with respect to resource deposits in the Area which lie across limits of national jurisdiction, shall be conducted with due regard to the rights and legitimate interests of any coastal State across whose jurisdiction such deposits lie.

# SECTION 3. DEVELOPMENT OF RESOURCES OF THE AREA

## Article 150

### Policies relating to activities in the Area

Activities in the Area shall, as specifically provided for in this Part, be carried out in such a manner as to foster healthy development of the world economy and balanced growth of international trade, and to promote international cooperation for the over-all development of all countries, especially developing States, and with a view to ensuring:

(a) the development of the resources of the Area;

(b) orderly, safe and rational management of the resources of the Area, including the efficient conduct of activities in the Area and, in accordance with sound principles of conservation, the avoidance of unnecessary waste;

(c) the expansion of opportunities for participation in such activities consistent in particular with articles 144 and 148;

(d) participation in revenues by the Authority and the transfer of technology to the Enterprise and developing States as provided for in this Convention;

(e) increased availability of the minerals derived from the Area as needed in conjunction with minerals derived from other sources, to ensure supplies to consumers of such minerals;

(f) the promotion of just and stable prices remunerative to producers and fair to consumers for minerals derived both from the Area and from other sources, and the promotion of long-term equilibrium between supply and demand;

(g) the enhancement of opportunities for all States Parties, irrespective of their social and economic systems or geographical location, to participate in the development of the resources of the Area and the prevention of monopolization of activities in the Area;
(h) the protection of developing countries from adverse effects on their economies or on their export earnings resulting from a reduction in the price of an affected mineral, or in the volume of exports of that mineral, to the extent that such reduction is caused by activities in the Area, as provided in article 151;
(i) the development of the common heritage for the benefit of mankind as a whole; and
(j) conditions of access to markets for the imports of minerals produced from the resources of the Area and for imports of commodities produced from such minerals shall not be more favourable than the most favourable applied to imports from other sources.

## SECTION 4. THE AUTHORITY

## SUBSECTION A. GENERAL PROVISIONS

### Article 156
### Establishment of the Authority

1. There is hereby established the International Seabed Authority, which shall function in accordance with this Part.

2. All States Parties are ipso facto members of the Authority.

3. Observers at the Third United Nations Conference on the Law of the Sea who have signed the Final Act and who are not referred to in article 305, paragraph 1(c), (d), (e) or (f), shall have the right to participate in the Authority as observers, in accordance with its rules, regulations and procedures.

4. The seat of the Authority shall be in Jamaica.

5. The Authority may establish such regional centres or offices as it deems necessary for the exercise of its functions.

# PART XII. PROTECTION AND PRESERVATION OF THE MARINE ENVIRONMENT

## SECTION 1. GENERAL PROVISIONS

### Article 192
### General obligation

States have the obligation to protect and preserve the marine environment.

### Article 193
### Sovereign right of States to exploit their natural resources

States have the sovereign right to exploit their natural resources pursuant to their environmental policies and in accordance with their duty to protect and preserve the marine environment.

### Article 194
### Measures to prevent, reduce and control pollution of the marine environment

1. States shall take, individually or jointly as appropriate, all measures consistent with this Convention that are necessary to prevent, reduce and control pollution of the marine environment from any source, using for this purpose the best practicable means at their disposal and in accordance with their capabilities, and they shall endeavour to harmonize their policies in this connection.

2. States shall take all measures necessary to ensure that activities under their jurisdiction or control are so conducted as not to cause damage by pollution to other States and their environment, and that pollution arising from incidents or activities under their jurisdiction or control does not spread beyond the areas where they exercise sovereign rights in accordance with this Convention.

3. The measures taken pursuant to this Part shall deal with all sources of pollution of the marine environment. These measures shall include, inter alia, those designed to minimize to the fullest possible extent:

(a) the release of toxic, harmful or noxious substances, especially those which are persistent, from land-based sources, from or through the atmosphere or by dumping;

(b) pollution from vessels, in particular measures for preventing accidents and dealing with emergencies, ensuring the safety of operations at sea, preventing intentional and unintentional discharges, and regulating the design, construction, equipment, operation and manning of vessels;

(c) pollution from installations and devices used in exploration or exploitation of the natural resources of the seabed and subsoil, in particular measures for preventing accidents and dealing with emergencies, ensuring the safety of operations at sea, and regulating the design, construction, equipment, operation and manning of such installations or devices;

(d) pollution from other installations and devices operating in the marine environment, in particular measures for preventing accidents and dealing with emergencies, ensuring the safety of operations at sea, and regulating the design, construction, equipment, operation and manning of such installations or devices.

4. In taking measures to prevent, reduce or control pollution of the marine environment, States shall refrain from unjustifiable interference with activities carried out by other States in the exercise of their rights and in pursuance of their duties in conformity with this Convention.

5. The measures taken in accordance with this Part shall include those necessary to protect and preserve rare or fragile ecosystems as well as the habitat of depleted, threatened or endangered species and other forms of marine life.

Article 195

Duty not to transfer damage or hazards or transform one type of pollution into another

In taking measures to prevent, reduce and control pollution of the marine environment, States shall act so as not to transfer, directly or indirectly, damage or hazards from one area to another or transform one type of pollution into another.

Article 196

Use of technologies or introduction of alien or new species

1. States shall take all measures necessary to prevent, reduce and control pollution of the marine environment resulting from the use of technologies under their jurisdiction or control, or the intentional or accidental introduction of species, alien or new, to a particular part of the marine environment, which may cause significant and harmful changes thereto.

2. This article does not affect the application of this Convention regarding the prevention, reduction and control of pollution of the marine environment.

Article 204

Monitoring of the risks or effects of pollution

1. States shall, consistent with the rights of other States, endeavour, as far as practicable, directly or through the competent international organizations, to observe, measure, evaluate and analyse, by recognized scientific methods, the risks or effects of pollution of the marine environment.

2. In particular, States shall keep under surveillance the effects of any activities which they permit or in which they engage in order to determine whether these activities are likely to pollute the marine environment.

# BIBLIOGRAPHY

All website links were correct as of 11 July 2023.


Akashi, Kinji, *Cornelius Van Bynkershoek: His Role in the History of International Law* (Boston: Kluwer Law International, 1998)

Amery, L. S., *My Political Life*, Vol. 2, *War and Peace 1914–29* (London: Hutchinson, 1953)

Anand, R. P., *Origin and Development of the Law of the Sea* (Dordrecht: Martinus Nijhoff Publishers, 1982)

Andermann, Jens, *Argentine Literature and the 'Conquest of the Desert', 1872–1896* (London: Birkbeck, University of London, n.d.)

Atkins, Scott, 'The Commercialisation of Outer Space', *International Corporate Rescue*, 19, No. 3 (2022), https://www.nortonrosefulbright.com/en/knowledge/publications/102a426e/the-commercialisation-of-outer-space#:~:text=Commercial%20space%20activity%20grew%206.6,of%20the%20total%20space%20economy.&text=Morgan%20Stanley%20estimates%20that%20the,from%20USD%20%24350%20billion%20currently

Baldwin, Daniela Sampaio, 'Diplomatic Culture and Institutional Design: Analyzing Sixty Years of Antarctic Treaty Governance', *Anais da Academia Brasileira de Ciências* (*Annals of the Brazilian Academy of Sciences*), 94, Suppl. 1 (2022)

Billington, Ray Allen, *Westward Expansion: A History of the American Frontier*, 6th ed. (Albuquerque: University of New Mexico Press, 2001)

*Buenos Aires Times*, 'Argentina Cancels Agreement with United Kingdom, Re-asserts Malvinas Sovereignty Claim', 2 March 2023, https://batimes.com.ar/news/argentina/argentina-cancels-agreement-with-uk-re-asserts-malvinas-sovereignty.phtml

Clarke, Arthur C., *The Exploration of Space* (New York: Harper Collins, 1951)

Cohen, Benjamin, *International Political Economy: An Intellectual History* (Princeton: Princeton University Press, 2008)

COPUOS (Committee on the Peaceful Uses of Outer Space), 65th Session, Report of the Legal Subcommittee, Vienna, 28 March–8 April 2022, https://www.unoosa.org/oosa/en/ourwork/copuos/lsc/2022/index.html

Corgan, Michael, 'US Ratification of UNCLOS III?', *E-International Relations*, 31 May 2012, https://www.e-ir.info/2012/05/31/us-ratification-of-unclos-iii/

Dolman, Everett C., 'Space is a Warfighting Domain', *Aether: A Journal of Strategic Airpower and Spacepower*, 1, No. 1 (2022), 82–90, https://www.airuniversity.af.edu/Portals/10/AEtherJournal/Journals/Volume-1_Issue-1/11-Dolman.pdf

Doyle, Stephen, 'A Concise History of Space Law', in Stephan Hobe (ed.), *Six Decades of Space Law and Its Development* (Paris: International Institute for Space Law, 2020)

Dreibus, G., et al., 'Lithium and Halogens in Lunar Samples', *Philosophical Transactions of the Royal Society of London, Series A, Mathematical and Physical Sciences*, 285, No. 1327 (1977), 49–54

*Economist*, 'Which Firm Will Win the New Moon Race?', 20 April 2023, https://www.economist.com/science-and-technology/2023/01/18/which-firm-will-win-the-new-moon-race?utm-campaign=r.the-economist-today&utm-medium=email.internal-newsletter.np&utm-source=salesforce-marketing-cloud&utm-term=4/20/2023&utm-id=1569516

European Space Agency, 'Types of Orbits', 30 March 2020, https://www.esa.int/Enabling_Support/Space_Transportation/Types_of_orbits

Federal Aviation Administration, United States Department of Transportation, 'Payload Reviews', https://www.faa.gov/space/licenses/payload_reviews

Gillett, Stephen L., 'The Value of the Moon', *L5News*, National Space Society, August 1983, https://space.nss.org/l5-news-the-value-of-the-moon/#:~:text=And%20the%20Moon%20may%20also,%2C%20tantalum%2C%20and%20so%20forth

Grayling, A. C., *The Frontiers of Knowledge* (London: Viking Penguin, 2021)

— *For the Good of the World* (London: Oneworld, 2022)

Grotius, Hugo, *Mare Liberum* ['The Freedom of the Seas'], trans. Ralph van Deman Magoffin (New York: Oxford University Press, 1916), https://oll.libertyfund.org/title/scott-the-freedom-of-the-seas-latin-and-english-version-magoffin-trans

Grover, Velma I., *Water: A Source of Conflict or Cooperation?* (Enfield, NH: Science Publishers, 2007)

Groves, Steven, 'The US Can Mine the Deep Seabed Without Joining the UN Convention on the Law of the Sea', *Heritage Foundation*, 4 December 2012, https://www.heritage.org/report/the-us-can-mine-the-deep-seabed-without-joining-the-un-convention-the-law-the-sea

Grunert, Jeremy, *The United States Space Force and the Future of American Space Policy: Legal and Policy Implications*, Studies in Space Law, Vol. 18 (Leiden: Brill Nijhoff, 2022)

Grush, Loren, 'US and Seven Other Countries Sign NASA's Artemis Accords to Set Rules for Exploring the Moon', *The Verge*, 13 October 2020, https://www.theverge.com/2020/10/13/21507204/nasa-artemis-accords-8-countries-moon-outer-space-treaty

Harvey, Chelsea, 'China and Russia Continue to Block Protections for Antarctica', *E&E News*, 29 November 2022, https://www.scientificamerican.com/article/china-and-russia-continue-to-block-protections-for-antarctica/

He, H. et al., 'A Solar Wind-Derived Water Reservoir on the Moon Hosted by Impact Glass Beads', *Nature Geoscience*, 16 (2023), 294–300, https://www.nature.com/articles/s41561-023-01159-6

Hobe, Stephan (ed.), *Pioneers of Space Law* (Leiden and Boston: Martinus Nijhoff, 2014)

— 'Taking Stock of the Development of Space Law After Half a Century', in Stephan Hobe (ed.), *Six Decades of Space Law and Its Development* (Paris: International Institute for Space Law, 2020)

Hooper, Craig, 'With New Gear and Bases, China Is Beginning to Make a Play for Dominance in Antarctica', *Forbes*, 23 December 2020, https://www.forbes.com/sites/craighooper/2020/12/23/big-antarctic-stakeholders-get-ignored-as-chinas-new-antarctic-gear-gets-hyped/?sh=273dfb2e52ea

International Court of Justice, 'Antarctica (United Kingdom v. Chile): Press Releases', https://www.icj-cij.org/case/27/press-releases

International Seabed Authority, 'Written Evidence (UNC0026) to the International Relations and Defence Committee', 11 November 2021, https://committees.parliament.uk/writtenevidence/40854/html/

International Union for Conservation of Nature, 'Issues Brief: Deep Sea Mining', May 2022, https://www.iucn.org/resources/issues-brief/deep-sea-mining

Jones, Andrew, 'China Recovers Chang'e-5 Moon Samples After Complex 23-day Mission', *Space News*, 16 December 2020, https://spacenews.com/china-recovers-change-5-Moon-Ssamples-after-Complex-23-day-Mission/

Justinian, *The Institutes*, The Latin Library, https://thelatinlibrary.com/law/institutes.html

Korovine, Eugène [Yevgeny Korovin], 'La conquête de la stratosphère et le droit international' ['The Conquest of the Stratosphere and International Law'], *Revue Générale de Droit International Public*, XLI (1934), 675–86

Krasner, Stephen, 'Think Again: Sovereignty', *Foreign Policy*, 20

November 2009, https://foreignpolicy.com/2009/11/20/think-again-sovereignty/

Laude, E., 'Questions Pratiques', Vol. 1, *Revue Juridique Internationale de Locomotion Aérienne,* 16–18, Paris (1910), translated into English as NASA Technical Memorandum NASA TM 77513, Washington, DC, August 1984

Leonard, David, 'Mining the Moon? Space Property Rights Still Unclear, Experts Say', *Space.com,* 25 July 2014, https://www.space.com/26644-moon-asteroids-resources-space-law.html

Livingstone, D., and C. Livingstone, *Narrative of an Expedition to the Zambesi and Its Tributaries: And of the Discovery of the Lakes Shirwa and Nyassa. 1858–1864* (New York: Harper & Brothers, 1866)

Locke, John, *Second Treatise of Government* (1689)

Lodge, Michael, 'The International Seabed Authority and Deep Seabed Mining', *Our Ocean, Our World,* Volumes 1 & 2, *UN Chronicle,* Vol. 54, May 2017, https://www.un.org/en/chronicle/article/international-seabed-authority-and-deep-seabed-mining

Lundgren, Magnus, et al., 'Stability and Change in International Policy -Making: A Punctuated Equilibrium Approach', *Review of International Organizations,* 13 (2018), 547–72

Mandl, Vladimir, *Problem Mezihvezdne Dopravy* ['The Problem of Interstellar Transport'] (Prague, 1932), quoted in Stephan Hobe (ed.), *Pioneers of Space Law* (Leiden and Boston: Martinus Nijhoff, 2014)

Martinez, L. F., 'Uses of Cyber Space and Space Law', in Stephan Hobe (ed.), *Six Decades of Space Law and Its Development* (Paris: International Institute for Space Law, 2020)

Mero, John L., *The Mineral Resources of the Sea* (Amsterdam: Elsevier, 1965)

Moore, John Norton, 'Statement of John Norton Moore: Senate Advice and Consent to the Law of the Sea Convention: Urgent Unfinished Business', Testimony before the Senate Foreign Relations Committee, 14 October 2003

Moskowitz, Clara, Lee Billings, and Kelso Harper, 'A Mission to Jupiter's Strange Moons Is Finally on Its Way', *Scientific American,* 19 April

2023, https://www.scientificamerican.com/podcast/episode/a-mission-to-jupiters-strange-moons-is-finally-on-its-way/

NASA (National Aeronautics and Space Administration), 'Artemis', https://www.nasa.gov/specials/artemis/

*Nature*, 'Editorial: Reform the Antarctic Treaty', 13 June 2018, https://www.nature.com/articles/d41586-018-05368-7

*New York Times*, 'Ispace Loses Contact with Moon Lander. Here's What Happened', 25 April 2023, https://www.nytimes.com/live/2023/04/25/science/ispace-moon-landing-japan

*New York Times*, 'What Happened During Ispace's Moon Landing Attempt', 25 April 2023, https://www.nytimes.com/live/2023/04/25/science/ispace-moon-landing-japan

Nolan, Frederick, *The Wild West: History, Myth, and the Making of America* (London: Arcturus, 2003)

Pakenham, Thomas, *The Scramble for Africa, 1876–1912* (London: Weidenfeld and Nicolson, 1991)

Rauch, G. V., *Conflict in the Southern Cone: The Argentine Military and the Boundary Dispute with Chile, 1870–1902* (Westport: Praeger, 1999)

Reid, Richard J., *A History of Modern Africa: 1800 to the Present*, 3rd ed. (Oxford: Wiley-Blackwell, 2020)

Rosenberg, Matt, 'The Berlin Conference to Divide Africa: The Colonisation of the Continent by European Powers', *Thoughtco.com*, 30 June 2019, https://www.thoughtco.com/berlin-conference-1884-1885-divide-africa-1433556

Roth, K. M., *Annihilating Difference: The Anthropology of Genocide* (Oakland: University of California Press, 2002)

Sanderson, G. N., 'The European Partition of Africa: Origins and Dynamics', in Roland Oliver and G. N. Sanderson (eds), *The Cambridge History of Africa*, Vol. 6 (Cambridge: Cambridge University Press, 1985)

Sands, Leo, and Dino Grandoni, 'Nations Agree on "World-Changing" Deal to Protect Ocean Life', *Washington Post*, 5 March 2023, https://www.washingtonpost.com/climate-environment/2023/03/05/un-ocean-treaty-high-seas/

Selden, John, *Mare Clausum Seu, De Dominio Maris* ['Of the Dominion or Ownership of the Seas'], trans. Marchamont Nedham (London: William Du-Gard, 1652), https://archive.org/details/ofdominionorowne00seld

Stilwell, Sean, 'Slavery in African History', in Sean Stilwell, *Slavery and Slaving in African History* (Cambridge: Cambridge University Press, 2013)

Thucydides, *The Peloponnesian War* (New York: Random House, 1951)

Truman, Harry S., 'United States Presidential Proclamation No. 2667 – Policy of the United States with Respect to the Natural Resources of the Subsoil and Sea Bed of the Continental Shelf', 28 September 1945, *The American Presidency Project*, https://www.presidency.ucsb.edu/documents/proclamation-2667-policy-the-united-states-with-respect-the-natural-resources-the-subsoil

United Nations, 'Dispute between Argentina and Chile Concerning the Beagle Channel', *Reports of International Arbitral Awards*, XXI (1977), 53–264, https://legal.un.org/riaa/cases/vol_XXI/53-264.pdf

— United Nations Convention on the Law of the Sea, 1982, http://www.un.org/depts/los/convention_agreements/texts/unclos/unclos_e.pdf

— 'Beyond Borders: Why New "High Seas" Treaty Is Critical for the World', *UN News*, 19 June 2023, https://news.un.org/en/story/2023/06/1137857

United Nations, Division for Ocean Affairs and the Law of the Sea, 'The United Nations Convention on the Law of the Sea (A Historical Perspective)', 1998, http://www.un.org/Depts/los/convention_agreements/convention_historical_perspective.htm#Third%20Conferen%20ce

United Nations, General Assembly, 'Resolution 1721 (XVI). International Co-operation in the Peaceful Uses of Outer Space', 1961, https://www.unoosa.org/oosa/en/ourwork/spacelaw/treaties/resolutions/res_16_1721.html#:~:text=(a)%20International%20law%2C%20including,2

— 'Declaration of Principles Governing the Sea-Bed and the Ocean Floor, and the Subsoil Thereof, beyond the Limits of National

Jurisdiction', 25th session, 1970, https://digitallibrary.un.org/record/201718?ln=en#record-files-collapse-header

United Nations, Office for Outer Space Affairs, Committee on the Peaceful Uses of Outer Space, https://www.unoosa.org/oosa/en/ourwork/copuos/index.html

United States Congress, 'S.3729 – 111th Congress (2009–2010): National Aeronautics and Space Administration Authorization Act of 2010', *Congress.gov*, Library of Congress, 11 October 2010, https://www.congress.gov/bill/111th-congress/senate-bill/3729

United States STARCOM (Space Force, Space Training and Readiness Command), *Space Doctrine Publication 4-0: Sustainment, Doctrine for Space Forces*, December 2022, https://www.starcom.spaceforce.mil/Portals/2/SDP%204-0%20Sustainment%20(Signed).pdf?ver=jFc_4BiAkDjJdc49LmESgg%3D%3D#:~:text=United%20States%20Space%20Force%20(USSF,of%20a%20broader%20joint%20force

Valantin, Jean-Michel, 'Antarctic China (1): Strategies for a Very Cold Place', Red Team Analysis Society, 31 May 2021, https://redanalysis.org/2021/05/31/antarctic-china-1-strategies-for-a-very-cold-place/

van der Post, Laurens, *Venture to the Interior* (London: Hogarth Press, 1952)

Verne, Jules, *Twenty Thousand Leagues Under the Seas*, translated by William Butcher (Oxford: Oxford University Press, 2019)

Vienna Convention on the Law of Treaties (1969), https://legal.un.org/ilc/texts/instruments/english/conventions/1_1_1969.pdf

Wall, Mike, 'Moon Mining Idea Digs up Lunar Legal Issues', *Space.com*, 14 January 2011, https://www.space.com/10621-moon-mining-legal-issues.html

Weingast, B. R., 'Rational Choice Institutionalism', in Ira Katznelson and Helen V. Milner (eds), *Political Science: The State of the Discipline* (New York: Norton, 2002), https://www.researchgate.net/publication/259953065_Rational_Choice_Institutionalism

*Wikipedia*, 'Boeing X-20 Dyna-Soar', https://en.wikipedia.org/wiki/Boeing_X-20_Dyna-Soar

Witz, Alexandre, 'Private Companies are Flocking to the Moon', *Nature*, 18 April 2023, https://www.nature.com/articles/d41586-023-01045-6?utm_source=Nature+Briefing&utm_campaign=5079b177e1-briefing-dy-20230419&utm_medium=email&utm_term=0_c9dfd39373-5079b177e1-45972542

Zarzar, V. A., 'Mezhdunarodnoye Publichnoye Vozdushnoye Pravo' ['Public International Air Law'], in *Voprosy Vozdushnogo Prava, Sportnik Trudov Sektsii Vozdushnogo Prava Soyuza Aviyakhim (Soyuz Obshchestv Druzhey Aviatsionnoy i Khimicheskoy Oborony i Promyshlennosti)* [*Problems of Air Law, a Symposium of Works by the Air Law Sections of the USSR and RSFSR Unions of Societies for Assisting Defense and Aviation and Chemical Construction*], Vol. 1 (Moscow: SSSR i Aviakhim RSFSR, 1927)

Zhukov, Gennady P., Vladlen S. Vereshchetin, and Anatoly Y. Kapustin, 'Evgeny Aleksandrovich Korovin (12.10.1892–3.11.1964)', in Stephan Hobe (ed.), *Pioneers of Space Law* (Leiden and Boston: Martinus Nijhoff, 2014)

# NOTES

## Preface

1 An example of the valuable work likely to be accessed only by specialists is Mai'a K. Davis Cross and Saadia M. Pekkanen 'Introduction: Space Diplomacy, The Final Frontier of Theory and Practice', *The Hague Journal of Diplomacy*, March 2023.

2 Alexandra Witze, 'Private Companies are Flocking to the Moon', *Nature*, 18 April 2023, https://www.nature.com/articles/d41586-023-01045-6?utm_source=Nature+Briefing&utm_campaign=5079b177e1-briefing-dy-20230419&utm_medium=email&utm_term=0_c9dfd39373-5079b177e1-45972542.

3 Ibid.

4 *Economist*, 'Which Firm Will Win the New Moon Race?', 20 April 2023, https://www.economist.com/science-and-technology/2023/01/18/which-firm-will-win-the-new-moon-race?utm_campaign=r.the-economist-today&utm_medium=email.internal-newsletter.np&utm_source=salesforce-marketing-cloud&utm_term=4/20/2023&utm_id=1569516.

## Introduction

1 Scott Atkins, 'The Commercialisation of Outer Space', *International Corporate Rescue*, 19, No. 3 (2022), https://www.nortonrosefulbright.com/en/knowledge/publications/102a426e/the-commercialisation-of-outer-space#:~:text=Commercial%20space%20activity%20grew%206.6,of%20the%20total%20space%20economy.&text=Morgan%20Stanley%20estimates%20that%20the,from%20USD%20%24350%20billion%20currently.

2 As these words were written, the European Space Agency's 'Juice' (Jupiter Icy Moons Explorer) spacecraft was *en route* to orbit around the giant planet: Clara Moskowitz, Lee Billings and Kelso Harper, 'A Mission to Jupiter's Strange Moons Is Finally on Its Way', *Scientific American*, 19 April 2023, https://www.scientificamerican.com/podcast/episode/a-mission-to-jupiters-strange-moons-is-finally-on-its-way/.

## 1 'Global Commons' and the Inheritance of Humanity

1 After several less successful attempts to bring the *Dune* story to the large and small screens, including one by David Lynch, the 2021 adaptation for cinema by Denis Villeneuve won plaudits. It covers the first half of the first *Dune* novel.

2 G. Dreibus et al., 'Lithium and Halogens in Lunar Samples', *Philosophical Transactions of the Royal Society of London, Series A, Mathematical and Physical Sciences*, 285, No. 1327 (1977), 49–54.

3 NASA found dozens of craters ranging in diameter from two to fifteen kilometres containing water ice, and estimated that there could be more than 600 million metric tons of water on the moon, much of it easily accessible. Subsequently, in March 2023, it was

announced in *Nature Geoscience*, following analysis of surface materials retrieved by China's Chang'e 5 lunar lander, that 270 *billion* tons of water might be held in impact glass beads on the lunar surface. See Huicun He et al., 'A Solar Wind-Derived Water Reservoir on the Moon Hosted by Impact Glass Beads', *Nature Geoscience*, 16 (2023), 294–300, https://www.nature.com/articles/s41561-023-01159-6.

4 Mike Wall, 'Moon Mining Idea Digs up Lunar Legal Issues', *Space.com*, 14 January 2011, https://www.space.com/10621-moon-mining-legal-issues.html.

5 Others include Lunar Outpost of Golden, Colorado; Masten Space Systems of Mojave, California; ispace Europe of Luxembourg; and ispace Japan of Tokyo.

6 David Leonard, 'Mining the Moon? Space Property Rights Still Unclear, Experts Say', *Space.com*, 25 July 2014, https://www.space.com/26644-moon-asteroids-resources-space-law.html.

7 Federal Aviation Administration, United States Department of Transportation, 'Payload Reviews', https://www.faa.gov/space/licenses/payload_reviews.

8 'Near space' is – roughly speaking, because definitions differ – the region between the 'Armstrong Limit' and the 'Kármán Line', the former being the altitude at which atmospheric pressure is such that human blood boils, about 60,000 feet (or eighteen kilometres above mean sea level), and the latter serving as the boundary between near and outer space, 100 kilometres above mean sea level, a significant altitude for required escape velocities of spacecraft. The lowest of 'low earth' satellite orbits are above the Kármán Line, at an altitude of 120 kilometres up to 1,000 kilometres. Most satellites, over seventy per cent of them, orbit in this range. Because Earth's gravity is significant at these altitudes, Low Earth Orbits (LEOs) cannot be maintained indefinitely. For comparison and completeness: a Medium Earth Orbit is generally about 20,000 kilometres above Earth's surface and a High Earth Orbit is generally about 35,000 kilometres up. Only two per cent of satellites orbit in this latter range. The moon's orbit is over ten times greater,

at an average distance from Earth of 382,500 kilometres (at perigee – the nearest distance – 360,000 kilometres).

See European Space Agency, 'Types of Orbits', 30 March 2020, https://www.esa.int/Enabling_Support/Space_Transportation/Types_of_orbits.

9 The texts of the relevant treaties and associated documents occur as Appendices 1–3 in this book.

10 Appendix 1.

11 The deep-sea bed wasn't an issue until, from the 1950s onwards, technological developments made it increasingly accessible to commercial-industrial exploitation.

12 United Nations General Assembly, 'Declaration of Principles Governing the Sea-Bed and the Ocean Floor, and the Subsoil Thereof, beyond the Limits of National Jurisdiction', 25th session, 1970, https://digitallibrary.un.org/record/201718?ln=en#record-files-collapse-header.

13 Justinian, *The Institutes*, The Latin Library, https://thelatinlibrary.com/law/institutes.html.

14 Ibid., Book II, Division I, §1–6, *passim*.

15 United Nations Convention on the Law of the Sea, 1982, http://www.un.org/depts/los/convention_agreements/texts/unclos/unclos_e.pdf, Preamble, and Section 2, Articles 136 and 137.

16 Leo Sands and Dino Grandoni, 'Nations Agree on "World-Changing" Deal to Protect Ocean Life', *Washington Post*, 5 March 2023, https://www.washingtonpost.com/climate-environment/2023/03/05/un-ocean-treaty-high-seas/.

17 John Locke, *Second Treatise of Government* (1689).

18 Velma I. Grover, *Water: A Source of Conflict or Cooperation?* (Enfield, NH: Science Publishers, 2007).

## 2 Protecting the Antarctic

1 Daniela Sampaio Baldwin, 'Diplomatic Culture and Institutional Design: Analyzing Sixty Years of Antarctic Treaty Governance',

*Anais da Academia Brasileira de Ciências* ('Annals of the Brazilian Academy of Sciences'), 94, Suppl. 1 (2022).

2 A foundational figure in regime theory is Stephen Krasner; see e.g. 'Think Again: Sovereignty', *Foreign Policy*, 20 November 2009, https://foreignpolicy.com/2009/11/20/think-again-sovereignty/, and Benjamin J. Cohen, *International Political Economy: An Intellectual History* (Princeton: Princeton University Press, 2008).

3 B. R. Weingast, 'Rational Choice Institutionalism', in Ira Katznelson and Helen V. Milner (eds), *Political Science: The State of the Discipline* (New York: Norton, 2002), https://www.researchgate.net/publication/259953065_Rational_Choice_Institutionalism, pp. 660 *et seq.*

4 Magnus Lundgren et al., 'Stability and Change in International Policy-Making: A Punctuated Equilibrium Approach', *Review of International Organizations*, 13 (2018), 547–72.

5 G. V. Rauch, *Conflict in the Southern Cone: The Argentine Military and the Boundary Dispute with Chile, 1870–1902* (Westport: Praeger, 1999).

6 Jens Andermann, *Argentine Literature and the 'Conquest of the Desert', 1872–1896* (London: Birkbeck, University of London, n.d.).

7 K. M. Roth, *Annihilating Difference: The Anthropology of Genocide* (Oakland: University of California Press, 2002), p. 45.

8 United Nations, 'Dispute between Argentina and Chile Concerning the Beagle Channel', *Reports of International Arbitral Awards*, XXI (1977), 53–264, https://legal.un.org/riaa/cases/vol_XXI/53-264.pdf.

9 *Buenos Aires Times*, 'Argentina Cancels Agreement with United Kingdom, Re-asserts Malvinas Sovereignty Claim', 2 March 2023, https://batimes.com.ar/news/argentina/argentina-cancels-agreement-with-uk-re-asserts-malvinas-sovereignty.phtml.

10 L. S. Amery, *My Political Life*, Vol. 2, *War and Peace 1914–29* (London: Hutchinson, 1953).

11 Hunter Christie was in Argentina during the presidency of Juan Perón.

12 A quarter of a century later Hunter Christie became a leading figure in the campaign to support Falkland Islander determination to remain British, a campaign prompted by the fact that, during the pre-Margaret Thatcher period of imperial disengagement, successive British governments had become more inclined to agree to Argentinian demands.
13 International Court of Justice, 'Antarctica (United Kingdom v. Chile): Press Releases', https://www.icj-cij.org/case/27/press-releases.
14 *Nature*, 'Editorial: Reform the Antarctic Treaty', 13 June 2018, https://www.nature.com/articles/d41586-018-05368-7.
15 Jean-Michel Valantin, 'Antarctic China (1): Strategies for a Very Cold Place', Red Team Analysis Society, 31 May 2021, https://redanalysis.org/2021/05/31/antarctic-china-1-strategies-for-a-very-cold-place/.
16 Craig Hooper, 'With New Gear and Bases, China Is Beginning to Make a Play for Dominance in Antarctica', *Forbes*, 23 December 2020, https://www.forbes.com/sites/craighooper/2020/12/23/big-antarctic-stakeholders-get-ignored-as-chinas-new-antarctic-gear-gets-hyped/?sh=273dfb2e52ea.
17 Chelsea Harvey, 'China and Russia Continue to Block Protections for Antarctica', *E&E News*, 29 November 2022, https://www.scientificamerican.com/article/china-and-russia-continue-to-block-protections-for-antarctica/.

## 3 High Seas and Deep Oceans

1 The Rhodian Law states the principle, applicable in insurance far beyond its marine applications, of 'general average', the proportionality shared by all stakeholders in a case of loss. The Law applied in particular to loss resulting from jettisoning some or all cargo to save a ship in distress.
2 Hugo Grotius, *Mare Liberum* ['The Freedom of the Seas'], trans.

Ralph van Deman Magoffin (New York: Oxford University Press, 1916), https://oll.libertyfund.org/title/scott-the-freedom-of-the-seas-latin-and-english-version-magoffin-trans.

3 John Selden, *Mare Clausum Seu, De Dominio Maris* ['Of the Dominion or Ownership of the Seas'], trans. Marchamont Nedham (London: William Du-Gard, 1652), https://archive.org/details/ofdominionorowne00seld.

4 Kinji Akashi, *Cornelius Van Bynkershoek: His Role in the History of International Law* (Boston: Kluwer Law International, 1998).

5 R. P. Anand, *Origin and Development of the Law of the Sea* (Dordrecht: Martinus Nijhoff Publishers, 1982), pp. 140–1. Although maritime issues were left unresolved, this conference had other important results, chief being agreements about matters of statelessness and nationality.

6 Harry S. Truman, 'United States Presidential Proclamation No. 2667 – Policy of the United States with Respect to the Natural Resources of the Subsoil and Sea Bed of the Continental Shelf', 28 September 1945, *The American Presidency Project*, https://www.presidency.ucsb.edu/documents/proclamation-2667-policy-the-united-states-with-respect-the-natural-resources-the-subsoil.

7 The call for a 'package deal' was made by Arvid Pardo, Malta's ambassador to the UN. United Nations, Division for Ocean Affairs and the Law of the Sea, 'The United Nations Convention on the Law of the Sea (A Historical Perspective)', 1998, http://www.un.org/Depts/los/convention_agreements/convention_historical perspective.htm#Third%20Conferen%20ce.

8 Michael Corgan, 'US Ratification of UNCLOS III?' *E-International Relations*, 31 May 2012, https://www.e-ir.info/2012/05/31/us-ratification-of-unclos-iii/.

9 The later sections of Part IX, viz. Sections 3–5, concern supervision of the regime established by Section 2, in the form of an Authority with competencies to carry out and enforce seabed governance.

10 John L. Mero, *The Mineral Resources of the Sea* (Amsterdam: Elsevier, 1965). 'The existence of mineral deposits in the deepest

parts of the ocean has been known since the 1860s. In Jules Verne's *Twenty Thousand Leagues Under the Sea,* Captain Nemo announced that "in the depths of the ocean, there are mines of zinc, iron, silver and gold that would be quite easy to exploit", predicting that the abundance of marine resources could satisfy human need. Although he was right about the abundance of the resources, he was most certainly wrong about how easy it would be to exploit them.' Michael Lodge, 'The International Seabed Authority and Deep Seabed Mining', *Our Ocean, Our World,* Volumes 1 & 2, *UN Chronicle,* Vol. 54, May 2017, https://www.un.org/en/chronicle/article/international-seabed-authority-and-deep-seabed-mining.

11 International Seabed Authority, 'Written Evidence (UNC0026) to the International Relations and Defence Committee', 11 November 2021, https://committees.parliament.uk/writtenevidence/40854/html/.

12 These arguments, and others, are summarised in Steven Groves, 'The US Can Mine the Deep Seabed Without Joining the UN Convention on the Law of the Sea', *Heritage Foundation,* 4 December 2012, https://www.heritage.org/report/the-us-can-mine-the-deep-seabed-without-joining-the-un-convention-the-law-the-sea.

13 John Norton Moore, 'Statement of John Norton Moore: Senate Advice and Consent to the Law of the Sea Convention: Urgent Unfinished Business', Testimony before the Senate Foreign Relations Committee, 14 October 2003.

14 United Nations Convention on the Law of the Sea, Annex III, 'Basic Conditions of Prospecting, Exploration and Exploitation', Article 13.

15 See International Union for Conservation of Nature, 'Issues Brief: Deep Sea Mining', May 2022, https://www.iucn.org/resources/issues-brief/deep-sea-mining.

16 United Nations Convention on the Law of the Sea, Annex VI, 'Statute of the International Tribunal for the Law of the Sea.'

17 As this book was about to be published, a legally binding marine biodiversity agreement, announced in late June 2023, was at last

reached by all 196 member states of the UN: United Nations, 'Beyond Borders: Why New "High Seas" Treaty Is Critical for the World', *UN News*, 19 June 2023, https://news.un.org/en/story/2023/06/1137857. As another step in the process of carrying international cooperation beyond mere aspiration it was a landmark moment. Any optimism it generates about a similar outcome in relation to further and better agreements governing human activity in outer space has to be qualified, however, for the obvious reason that whereas protecting the oceans' health is an essential component of efforts to manage the effects of global warming and humanity's part in it, outer space appears to offer no comparable environmental challenges – and therefore the pressure for a similar level of agreement and restraint is, to date anyway, far less.

## 4 The Scramble for Africa

1 A. C. Grayling, *The Frontiers of Knowledge* (London: Viking Penguin, 2021), pp. 204–7.
2 R. A. Billington, *Westward Expansion: A History of the American Frontier*, 6th ed. (Albuquerque: University of New Mexico Press, 2001); see also Frederick Nolan, *The Wild West: History, Myth, and the Making of America* (London: Arcturus, 2003).
3 The mythos of the 'Dark Continent' persisted. Laurens van der Post's book *Venture to the Interior* (London: Hogarth Press, 1952) exploited the idea in non-African minds that the interior of Africa is a trackless mystery, forbidding and even threatening; the book describes a 'remote part of Africa' which took quite some getting to – by air from London to Tripoli to Khartoum to Kampala to Nairobi to Lusaka to Salisbury (Harare) and thence finally to the city of Blantyre in his destination, Nyasaland (now Malawi). The book is a lyrical and charming account of the man, his antecedents, and his adventures on Mount Mlanje (now spelled Mulanje) and on the Nyika Plateau of northern Nyasaland high above great

Lake Nyasa (Lake Malawi) – more an inland sea than a lake – that gave the country its name after 'British Central Africa' had been carved into three parts: a colony, Southern Rhodesia (now Zimbabwe), and two 'protectorates', Northern Rhodesia (now Zambia) and Nyasaland.

The present author was born in the first of these protectorates and lived in the second of them. And that is the point: van der Post's thrilling and haunting experiences in the mists of Mount Mlanje relate to a place where the author went for picnics; it was a surprise to find, on reading this otherwise lovely book, that what was an hour's drive from home in Blantyre-Limbe through the tea estates of the Cholo ridge – whose steep terraces of tea bushes were twice annually soaked by fine drizzling rains blown from Mount Chiperone in Mozambique – was the dark heart of a dark continent. It was light enough to us.

4 D. Livingstone and C. Livingstone, *Narrative of an Expedition to the Zambesi and Its Tributaries: And of the Discovery of the Lakes Shirwa and Nyassa. 1858–1864* (New York: Harper & Brothers, 1866).

The Arab slave trade drew also on West Africa, captives being transported across the continent along the belt of savannah below the southern margin of the Sahara Desert, from Timbuktu to the Red Sea. There was a major slave market in Khartoum, and Arab purchases of African slaves continued into the twentieth century. See Sean Stilwell, 'Slavery in African History', in Sean Stilwell, *Slavery and Slaving in African History* (Cambridge: Cambridge University Press, 2013).

5 According to the legendary Chiripula Stephenson, the insistence by missionaries that Africans must at all times wear the European clothes they were given resulted in deaths because the items of apparel – a dress for the women, a shirt and pair of shorts for the men – were religiously kept on even when wet at night as their owners slept, with the result that they contracted chills leading to pneumonia; this claim was made in personal communication between Stephenson and the author's father. The claim is not entirely improbable, given that Africans might have lacked immunity to some of the diseases brought by missionaries; in the opposite direction, missionaries were of course far more susceptible to the tropical diseases that still abound in Africa.

6 G. N. Sanderson, 'The European Partition of Africa: Origins and Dynamics', in Roland Oliver and G. N. Sanderson (eds), *The Cambridge History of Africa,* Vol. 6 (Cambridge: Cambridge University Press, 1985), p. 99. This invaluable volume, together with Richard J. Reid, *A History of Modern Africa: 1800 to the Present,* 3rd ed. (Oxford: Wiley-Blackwell, 2020), and Thomas Pakenham, *The Scramble for Africa, 1876–1912* (London: Weidenfeld and Nicolson, 1991), are the sources for the account given here.

7 For a concise summary see Matt Rosenberg, 'The Berlin Conference to Divide Africa: The Colonisation of the Continent by European Powers', *Thoughtco.com,* 30 June 2019, https://www.thoughtco.com/berlin-conference-1884-1885-divide-africa-1433556.

8 Sanderson, 'European Partition', p. 97.

9 Ibid.

10 Ibid., p. 99.

11 Ibid., p. 102. Pakenham, *Scramble for Africa,* is informatively detailed on the ambitions in Africa of Belgium's King Leopold II and Germany's Prince Otto von Bismarck, who, until an apparently sudden change of mind in the early 1880s, had been opposed to German involvement in African colonisation.

12 Britain ended its partnership with France in dual control of Egypt through the Khedive's government, annoyed by France's unwillingness to pay its share of Egyptian debt, and anyway as part of Britain's non-negotiable determination to fortify all approaches to India through Suez, the Near East, Afghanistan, or round the Cape. See Pakenham, *Scramble for Africa,* Chapter 8, *passim.*

13 German South West Africa is now Namibia, having been under South African control following Germany's loss of it after 1918; and German East Africa is now Tanzania; after 1918 it became and remained until independence the British protectorate of Tanganyika.

14 Pakenham, *Scramble for Africa*; see note 6 above.

15 The Mahdists had risen against the inept rule of the Khedive of Egypt, whom the British controlled, but who had been left by

Britain to manage the Sudan, which it regarded as an unimportant sideshow.

16 Sanderson, 'European Partition', p. 113.
17 Ibid., p. 117.
18 Reid, *History*, p. 159.
19 Sanderson, 'European Partition', p. 119.
20 Ibid., p. 122.

## 5 Is the Outer Space Treaty Good Enough?

1 Thucydides, *The Peloponnesian War* (New York: Random House, 1951), p. 331.
2 E. Laude, 'Questions Pratiques', Vol. 1, *Revue Juridique Internationale de Locomotion Ariénne*, 16–18, Paris (1910), translated into English as NASA Technical Memorandum NASA TM 77513, Washington, DC, August 1984.
3 V. A. Zarzar, 'Mezhdunarodnoye Publichnoye Vozdushnoye Pravo' ['Public International Air Law'], in *Voprosy Vozdushnogo Prava, Sportnik Trudov Sektsii Vozdushnogo Prava Soyuza Aviyakhim (Soyuz Obshchestv Druzhey Aviatsionnoy i Khimicheskoy Oborony i Promyshlennosti)* [*Problems of Air Law, a Symposium of Works by the Air Law Sections of the USSR and RSFSR Unions of Societies for Assisting Defense and Aviation and Chemical Construction*], Vol. 1 (Moscow: SSSR i Aviakhim RSFSR, 1927).
4 Vladimir Mandl, *Problem Mezihvezdne Dopravy* ['The Problem of Interstellar Transport'] (Prague, 1932), quoted in Stephan Hobe (ed.), *Pioneers of Space Law* (Leiden and Boston: Martinus Nijhoff, 2014), Chapter V, *passim.*
5 Hobe (ed.), *Pioneers of Space Law*, p. 63.
6 General Assembly, 'Resolution 1721 (XVI). International Co-operation in the Peaceful Uses of Outer Space', 1961, https://www.unoosa.org/oosa/en/ourwork/spacelaw/treaties/

resolutions/res_16_1721.html#:~:text=(a)%20International%20law%2C%20including,2.

7 Ibid.

8 Ibid., pp. 63–4.

9 Ibid., p. 64.

10 Eugène Korovine [Yevgeny Korovin], 'La conquête de la stratosphère et le droit international' ['The Conquest of the Stratosphere and International Law'], *Revue Générale de Droit International Public*, XLI (1934), 675–86. See also Gennady P. Zhukov, Vladlen S. Vereshchetin and Anatoly Y. Kapustin, 'Evgeny Aleksandrovich Korovin (12.10.1892–3.11.1964)', in Stephan Hobe (ed.), *Pioneers of Space Law* (Leiden and Boston: Martinus Nijhoff, 2014).

11 Arthur C. Clarke, *The Exploration of Space* (New York: Harper Collins, 1951).

12 Stephen Doyle, 'A Concise History of Space Law', in Stephan Hobe (ed.), *Six Decades of Space Law and Its Development* (Paris: International Institute for Space Law, 2020), p. 9.

13 Ibid., p. 11.

14 Stephan Hobe, 'Taking Stock of the Development of Space Law after Half a Century', in Hobe (ed.), *Six Decades*, p. 46.

15 L. F. Martinez, 'Uses of Cyber Space and Space Law', in Hobe (ed.), *Six Decades*, pp. 51 *et seq.*

16 Quoted in ibid., p. 58.

17 Ibid., p. 59.

18 There was other equipment on board under test: an experimental solid-state battery made by NGK of Japan, an AI flight computer and a set of 360° cameras made by the Canadian aerospace contractor Canadensys Aerospace.

19 Andrew Jones, 'China Recovers Chang'e-5 Moon Samples after Complex 23-day Mission', *Space News*, 16 December 2020, https://spacenews.com/china-recovers-change-5-moon-samples-after-complex-23-day-mission/.

20 *New York Times*, 'Ispace Loses Contact with Moon Lander. Here's What Happened', 25 April 2023, https://www.nytimes.com/live/2023/04/25/science/ispace-moon-landing-japan.

21 See Loren Grush, 'US and Seven Other Countries Sign NASA's Artemis Accords to Set Rules for Exploring the Moon', *The Verge*, 13 October 2020, https://www.theverge.com/2020/10/13/21507204/nasa-artemis-accords-8-countries-moon-outer-space-treaty.

22 United States Congress, 'S.3729 – 111th Congress (2009–2010): National Aeronautics and Space Administration Authorization Act of 2010', *Congress.gov*, Library of Congress, 11 October 2010, https://www.congress.gov/bill/111th-congress/senate-bill/3729.

23 NASA, 'Artemis', https://www.nasa.gov/specials/artemis/.

24 United States STARCOM (Space Force, Space Training and Readiness Command), *Space Doctrine Publication 4-0: Sustainment, Doctrine for Space Forces*, December 2022, https://www.starcom.spaceforce.mil/Portals/2/SDP%204-0%20Sustainment%20(Signed).pdf?ver=jFc_4BiAkDjJdc49LmESgg%3D%3D#:~:text=United%20States%20Space%20Force%20(USSF,of%20a%20broader%20joint%20force.

25 Jeremy Grunert, *The United States Space Force and the Future of American Space Policy: Legal and Policy Implications*, Studies in Space Law, Vol. 18 (Leiden: Brill Nijhoff, 2022), p. 189.

26 Everett C. Dolman, 'Space is a Warfighting Domain', *Aether: A Journal of Strategic Airpower and Spacepower*, 1, No. 1 (2022), 82–90, https://www.airuniversity.af.edu/Portals/10/AEtherJournal/Journals/Volume-1_Issue-1/11-Dolman.pdf.

27 *Wikipedia*, 'Boeing X-20 Dyna-Soar', https://en.wikipedia.org/wiki/Boeing_X-20_Dyna-Soar.

28 United Nations, Office for Outer Space Affairs, Committee on the Peaceful Uses of Outer Space, https://www.unoosa.org/oosa/en/ourwork/copuos/index.html.

29 COPUOS (Committee on the Peaceful Uses of Outer Space), 65th Session, Report of the Legal Subcommittee, Vienna, 28 March–8 April 2022, https://documents-dds-ny.un.org/doc/UNDOC/GEN/V22/022/49/PDF/V2202249.pdf?OpenElement, para 222.

# Conclusion

1 An example is the announcement in February 2023 by President Vladimir Putin of Russia that he was suspending his country's participation in the New START Treaty (which limits the number of strategic nuclear warheads permitted in the armouries of the US and Russia) because of Western aid for Ukraine's resistance to Russia's invasion of that country.

2 One could cite slavery, poverty, harsh working conditions, inequality, injustice, environmental despoliation, and more, as concomitants of unregulated capitalism, all amply demonstrated by history. For just one less familiar example: the 1858 gold rush into the Pikes Peak area of the Rocky Mountains in Colorado resulted in Native Americans losing the lands guaranteed to them by the 1851 Fort Laramie treaty, extending over what are now the US states of Wyoming, Nebraska, Colorado, and Kansas. 'Wild West' conditions prevailed, fighting broke out between Native Americans and the invaders of their lands, atrocities were committed by both sides but those against Native Americans, as the example of the Sand Creek massacre shows, were especially egregious, and were followed by their eventual corralling into 'reservations' a tiny fraction of the size of the terrains they once roamed over.

See Grayling, *Frontiers of Knowledge*, pp. 204–5.

3 Agents are *legal persons* – this concept includes businesses and governments as well as individual human beings other than anyone too young or otherwise insufficiently mentally competent.

4 Vienna Convention on the Law of Treaties (1969), https://legal.un.org/ilc/texts/instruments/english/conventions/1_1_1969.pdf.

# INDEX

References to notes are indicated by n.